PELICAN
A916

TEACHING MACHINES AND PROGRAMMED INSTRUCTION

Professor Harry Kay has been head of the Psychology Department at the University of Sheffield since 1960. He is a Yorkshireman who went up to Trinity Hall, Cambridge, in 1938 but then spent the years 1939–45 in the Army. He returned to Cambridge in 1946 where he read Psychology and took his doctorate, before going as a lecturer to Oxford in 1951. He taught at Oxford until 1959 apart from one year spent in the United States as a Visiting Scientist at the National Institutes of Health. In 1967 the National Centre for Programmed Instruction for Industry was established in the Department of Psychology at Sheffield.

Bernard Dodd was born in London in 1934 but read Psychology in the University of Aberdeen where he gained a first class honours degree in 1962. For the last five years he has been engaged in research on programmed instruction and industrial training, and has published extensively in this field. In 1967 he became the Research Director of the P. I. Centre at Sheffield. He has wide interests and worked as a professional musician throughout his undergraduate career.

Max Sime, born in 1927, served in the R.A.F. before becoming an accounting machine engineer. During this period he studied Philosophy by attending W.E.A. evening lectures. On being awarded a Mature State Scholarship in 1957 he read Philosophy and Psychology at Balliol College, Oxford, and from that time has continued to work in psychological research. He has various technical publications in the fields of ageing and learning and teaching systems. His present research, which is supported by the Social Science Research Council, is on adaptive learning environments.

TEACHING MACHINES AND PROGRAMMED INSTRUCTION

HARRY KAY · BERNARD DODD

MAX SIME

PENGUIN BOOKS

Penguin Books Ltd, Harmondsworth, Middlesex, England
Penguin Books Inc., 3300 Clipper Mill Road, Baltimore, Md 21211, U.S.A.
Penguin Books Australia Ltd, Ringwood, Victoria, Australia

—

First published 1968

—

Copyright © Harry Kay, Bernard Dodd, Max Sime, 1968

—

Made and printed in Great Britain
by Richard Clay (The Chaucer Press) Ltd,
Bungay, Suffolk
Set in Monotype Times

CONTENTS

PREFACE

WHEN the authors first became interested in teaching machines about ten years ago, the subject was novel and expanding rapidly. Now the novelty has largely worn off but the expansion has continued. More people use programmed instruction now: more research workers are interested in developing its techniques: more practising teachers and instructors are interested in applying these techniques to their own teaching activities. This book has emphasized the relatively simple techniques of programming which most programmers use to begin with. But even since the manuscript was written there have been changes of emphasis and redeployments of resources so that were the book to be rewritten now it would turn out to be rather different. What has remained as an important anchor point has been the concept of a self-correcting system. Therefore, we are pleased to be able to report that the body of knowledge and skills known as Programmed Instruction is itself behaving like a self-correcting system in that it is adapting itself to changing circumstances. It is, for instance, taking account of the newer media such as film loops, closed circuit television, programmed broadcast television. It is also taking account of new developments in computer programming technology such as list-processing languages for small computers. The micro-fiche has arrived. And new topics for the new media are not hard to find – decimal currency and metrication are close at hand.

Now although as research workers we are interested in exploring new ways of applying programming techniques, we are only too well aware of the many facets of teaching which are not likely to be handed over to the pupil and his teaching machine. This is no panacea. Yet in its short history this area of teaching technology has had a remarkably widespread effect on all forms of teaching: not by any means in all schools and training centres, but we are frequently being surprised by descriptions of projects which embody some of the principles of programmed instruction.

Just about every form of teaching has succumbed in at least a handful of instances.

If we had to summarize the main effects we would certainly mention the increasing emphasis on statements of intent and evidence of accomplishment. Teachers are being increasingly precise in stating what their activities are intended to communicate: and they are becoming aware of the benefits to pupil and teacher of reliable measuring devices which will show which parts of the intended communications reached their destinations. As the educational world becomes more skilled at measuring what has been learned we confidently predict that the professionalism of our teachers and instructors will lead them to reconsider their results and to seek ways of improving them.

We hope that our predictions come true sooner than we had expected and that the experimental approach to teaching will become so familiar that future trainee teachers will have to refer to their history books to find out about the other way.

SELECTED BIBLIOGRAPHY

AUSTWICK, K. (1964). *Teaching Machines and Programming.* Oxford: Pergamon.

B.B.C. (1965). *What is Programmed Learning?* London: B.B.C.

BECKER, J. L. (1963). *A Programmed Guide to Writing Auto-instructional Programs.* New Jersey: Radio Corporation of America.

CAVANAGH, P. and JONES, C. (1966). *The Association for Programmed Learning Yearbook 1966–67. Programmes in Print.* London: Association for Programmed Learning.

COULSON, J. E. (1962). *Programmed Learning and Computer-based Instruction.* (Proceedings of the Conference on application of digital computers to automated instruction.) New York: Wiley.

DAVEY, D. M. and MCDONNELL, P. (1964). *Programmed Instruction.* Institute of Personnel Management.

DODD, B. T. (1967). *Programmed Instruction for Industrial Training.* London: Heinemann.

GOODMAN, R. (1965). *Programmed Learning and Teaching Machines. An introduction.* London: English University Press.

HENDERSHOT, C. H. (1965). *Programmed Learning – a Bibliography of Programmes and Presentation Devices.* 3rd edition. 1964–5 with supplements to October 1965. National Society for Programmed Instruction. Washington: National Education Association.

KAY, H., ANNETT, J. and SIME, M. E. (1963) *Teaching Machines and Their Use in Industry.* London: H.M.S.O.

LEITH, G. O. M. (1966). *A Handbook of Programmed Learning.* 2nd edition. Birmingham University: Institute of Education.

MARGULIES, S. and EIGEN, L. S. (eds.) (1962). *Applied Programmed Instruction.* New York: Wiley.

MARKLE, S. M. (1964). *Good Frames and Bad. A Grammar of Frame Writing.* New York: Wiley.

OFIESH, G. D. and MEIERHENRY, W. C. (eds.) (1964). *Trends in Programmed Instruction.* (Papers from the 1st annual convention of the National Society for Programmed Instruction.) Washington: National Education Association.

RICHMOND, W. K. (1967). *The Teaching Revolution.* London: Methuen.

ROWNTREE, D. (1966). *Basically Branching. A Handbook for Programmers.* London: MacDonald.

CHAPTER 1

WHAT ARE PROGRAMMES AND TEACHING MACHINES?

TEACHERS rarely watch teachers teaching. We all have been classroom pupils, perhaps long ago, but few of us go back and see teachers or teaching in action. Even so we have vivid memories of the classroom and assume things are much the same today. And alas, this is often true. Classes are about the same size – too big. Chalk and talk methods still dominate, and the syllabus trails along getting ever farther from this century and its unprecedented developments. Fortunately it is not our problem to try and explain why some subjects are respectable classroom material for children – why, say, history with its accounts of assassinations, blood-lettings on a gargantuan scale is considered a fit subject for tender minds whilst psychology with its account of how we see the world and adapt to it is not. But it is our aim to examine how subjects might be taught, and it is our contention that the introduction of some of the procedures we shall discuss will have beneficial repercussions upon established methods.

We wish to discuss certain ideas and methods that are offering something to teaching primarily because they belong to self-correcting systems. We believe in these methods, but whether they are good or bad need not be left to our or any pedagogue's opinion; they are open to scrutiny and amendment. If they do not work they must be rejected or modified, and one thing is definite – the objectives of the procedure can be specified and we can find out if they have been achieved. We accept that many of the aims of education are long term and that it is often difficult to say whether they have or have not been met. The danger here is that we may be accepting standards that are lower than we suspect. But we can make a humble beginning by agreeing about some of the things that we do wish to teach and examining how successful we have been. It is only too easy for discussions about teaching to get lost in the higher regions of educational aims and never be close to the nail-biting youngster in a classroom, the teenagers in the social competition of their school world, or a young apprentice in the hurly-burly of an adult industry. We are dealing with practical developments and so that we may have some picture of what we are to discuss, let us begin with a tour of some classrooms as they might look if they were using programmed instructions and teaching machines.

The children in this classroom are not sitting in rows of desks. Parts of the room have been divided off and through the partitions we can see machines, some of which from their size and screens look suspiciously like television sets. But when we open the door to one of these rooms we find the children are operating the machines themselves by pressing buttons and reading instructions on the screen. The machines make some noise and hence each cubicle is acoustically sheltered from the next. Each child is working on his own machine and at this point with little reference to a human teacher. In one part of the room there are study desks where students are working on their own although they can see and speak to their neighbours if they wish.

It is apparent that many different kinds of material are being used. One student has a small book. As he reads he writes occasionally on a pad beside the book. In fact he seems to write something at least once for every page and he frequently turns the pages, sometimes twice within the minute. His text is abundantly illustrated and he covers the pages rapidly. At the end he fills in a form which serves as a check that he has not missed anything. The next pupil also has a book, but he turns back and forth because he has to choose from a list of possible answers to the question which is at the bottom of almost every page. His choice leads him to a page which teaches him again if he has made a mistake or goes on to fresh material if he has chosen the correct answer. Yet another child has a textbook with a smaller companion book. This book is guiding him through the larger text by instruction and graded questions which he can answer by interpreting the text.

In another room someone is learning a keyboard skill for punch-card operators. He is obviously using a sophisticated machine for as we watch we realize that it is adapting its lesson to suit the moment to moment requirements of the learner. It soon repeats the problems where he had difficulty or went wrong, and speeds up presentation as he masters the task.

In a third classroom there are thirty student places, each with an individual screen on which lesson materials appear. At each place a student has a set of buttons so that he may record his responses. These are all transmitted to a control room in which there is a computer. It monitors the lessons of each of the thirty students, all of whom are at different stages in the course. It keeps records not only of how well each student is doing, but also of how well the lesson materials are teaching. From time to time the authors of these materials consult the computer for any difficulties in their programmes. The computer will print out a list on its teleprinter so that it is possible to see at a glance where students have been delayed and the kind of mistakes the programme has produced. The teacher rewrites the suspected passage and this is inserted in the programme.

Of course this kind of institution is still rare, but this is the direction we are taking. In this book we wish to show the reader the various ideas which lead there. Some of them lead to computer-based teaching systems, some to more homely devices which your children will bring back as part of their homework, which you yourself will pick up in the bookshops, and even the supermarkets, whenever you come upon something you would like to learn. We are going to discuss teaching machines and the ideas behind them, and above all we shall discuss programmed instruction where what the learner does in order to learn is closely controlled by something we call a programme. It is the programme which tells the student what to do, and where a teaching machine is involved, the programme will also tell it what to do.

Like so many of our modern inventions, a teaching machine on its own is neither good nor bad. It needs detailed instructions. And the art of programming is the art of gathering together many minds, teachers, subject-matter experts, educational technologists, and from their interaction producing something which will teach, and teach well, in the morning, after lunch, to slow learners, to fast, to white and to coloured.

Let us begin with a simple teaching programme in book form.

LINEAR PROGRAMMED BOOK

At present the most popular form of programme is the linear programmed book. It certainly can be made to teach. Some people say that a programmed book is a teaching machine in which the student himself takes the place of part of the machinery by obeying the instructions printed on the pages of the programme. A machine may move on the programme when you press the button; a book moves it on when you turn the page. A machine may allow you to skip over sections you do not need; the book will ask you to skip over certain pages where you do not need them.

The author of a programmed book has to write his frames so as to encourage a student to obey the instructions which will expedite his learning. When working with more elaborate machines the student's behaviour can be more closely controlled and he takes less responsibility. But with a programmed book one major issue is how to write a compelling text. How can we encourage a student to do whatever is necessary in order to learn?

Perhaps an example of a sequence from a linear programmed book will give the feel of this material better than a description. However, there are certain points to look for in the example. Notice how frequently the student is called upon to do something, generally once every frame. There are many ways of arranging these frames within a programmed book. Some are easier to use than others but may cost more to produce. This particular programme will probably be printed on separate pages of a small booklet with the correct answers for each frame on the reverse side of the page. This means that the student has the opportunity to think out and write down his response before he turns the page to find out whether his answer is correct. Notice also how easy the little tasks are if you have been working through the complete programme. If you get the wrong answer, it will almost certainly be because you have forgotten or not noticed, something. It will also be apparent to you that in this short extract you have missed some previous material and that some of the questions cannot be answered on the basis of this information alone. But try it for yourself; it is a section of programme from an engineering apprenticeship course.

This example is taken from a course in engineering craft practice, published by Empiric Ltd, Nottingham.* The programme has explained previously how a tensile test is conducted and how the test piece fractures.

FRAME	RESPONSE [Normally printed on reverse side]
33 Most engineering materials are slightly elastic or springy. So if the load is taken off before fracture occurs, a tensile test piece will usually: a) get longer b) stay the same c) get shorter	c) get shorter
34 Do all materials always go back to their original dimensions when the load is taken off?	No, not always
35 An elastic material .... (does/does not) return to its original dimensions.	does

* B. T. Dodd, 1965.

36	
A plastic material .... (does/does not) return to its original dimensions.	does not

37	
A material which returns to its original dimensions, even after having been highly stressed, is said to have .... (high/low) elasticity	high

38	
What is the formula for stress? [*This is a revision frame. The students have already been taught the formula.*]	$Stress = \dfrac{Load}{Area}$

39	
Which has low elasticity? (a) cast iron (b) phosphor-bronze	(a) Cast iron

40

What use is a metal with high elasticity?

Phosphor-bronze has high elasticity and is used for springs and flexible parts.

41

If you over-stress any material it .... (will/will not) return to its original dimensions when the load is removed.

will not

42

Stress depends on ....
and ....

Load
area

43

At a certain stress called the elastic limit, a particular material will begin to flow so that it will not return to its original dimensions when the load is removed.

What are the units of the elastic limit?

The elastic limit is a stress. Its units are tonf/in.^{2} or lbf/in.^{2} (tons force or lbs. force).

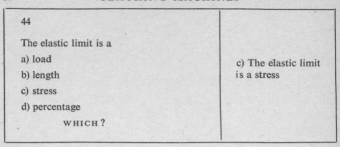

44

The elastic limit is a

a) load

b) length

c) stress

d) percentage

WHICH?

c) The elastic limit is a stress

   This programme has been designed to suit young people in the engineering industry or those preparing for it. The style is typical of linear programmes although many will use longer frames with more words than this. But you will agree that each frame is contributing to a very powerful control over what the student thinks and does whilst he reads. Words are not wasted. If the student can think out something for himself then the programme gives only a few cues to guide him. When the programme is first tried out (evaluated), if it is found that some students are unable to keep up the pace, the text is carefully modified to try and remove its defects without also destroying its good points. Since this programme was written for a particular type of student, we do not suggest it is suitable for a graduate scientist or the middle form of a girls' public school. The programme is intended for 15–16-year-old boys of average intelligence who want to be engineers. It is at an elementary level, but even so fairly advanced conceptual knowledge is built up from common data. You will notice also how the student is left in no doubt as to what he must do at each frame. He takes small steps, but they are taken surely and in the right direction. If engineering is not your subject then we did suggest you might experience some difficulty at one or two points with this short extract because you have missed earlier material that is relevant; for example, at frame 39 or 43, where you are called to use information that has previously been given in the text. It will be apparent that though the frames make only a small step forward each time, there is a definite sequence that the learner should follow. Conversely, where the programme has failed to give all the necessary steps the omission soon becomes patently obvious.

TEACHING MACHINES USING BRANCHING PROGRAMMES

By contrast with the linear programme where every student sees the same sequence of frames, the branching programme gets its name from the fact that extra frames (or branches) are provided for students who do not get the correct answer. Both types of programme can be used in book form or in a teaching machine, although the branching type is more attractive when presented by a machine because it can supply these extra frames without making the student turn back and forth.

With a linear book the student assesses his own answers and goes on to the next frame when satisfied, but a branching programme does not usually rely on the student to do his own marking. It provides a list of possible responses from which the student selects one. If he chooses the correct answer he is led to the next frame in the sequence, but if his choice was incorrect, he will be led to a 'wrong-answer frame' where the probable cause of his error is explained to him. He is then directed to return to the frame on which he went wrong in order to try again. In practice, one frame is usually enough to put the student in the picture again, although it is possible to include a sequence of frames for those who choose a particular wrong answer. If there are several types of wrong answer there will be a corresponding number of remedial frames or sequences.

You may well object that a multi-choice question allows the student to guess the correct answer. To provide for this contingency, the right-answer frames always include a short recapitulation covering the reasons or thought processes by which the right answer should have been obtained. All in all there are eight parts to a right-answer frame and six to a wrong. We will be brutal and list them: 1) frame number and indication of the previous frame in case the student loses his place 2) restatement of student's previous answer 3) indication of whether it was correct or not 4) explanation of why it was correct or not 5) new information or fresh explanation of point misunderstood 6) question 7) list of possible answers 8) routeing instructions so that the student will know where to go next. Now ask yourself the easy question, which two features are absent from a wrong-answer frame? Just because this is an ordinary book you may have been reading too quickly and find that you have to go over the list in order to get the answer. But right or wrong you should get a better feel for the situation if you look at the following example of a branching sequence.

The programme has already dealt with the history and background of programmed instruction and is a discussion of how a programme can teach pupils of different abilities.

FRAME 1

Some students will grasp a point quickly, others will need several repetitions and illustrative examples. In class, the teacher can ask questions and examine written work so as to determine how many of her class are ready to move on to the next point. But she cannot wait for everyone to understand without holding back those who grasp the point quickly. No matter what she does, there will be some students who are being made to work at a pace which does not suit them.

Programmed instruction can be arranged to allow each student to work at his own pace. This is called the Principle of Self-pacing.

Self-pacing means that

A. Every student will be able to get through the programme as quickly or as slowly as he pleases.

Press button A. (The machine will then show Frame 2.)

B. A student will be able to go on to fresh material as soon as he has understood the previous teaching, but not before.

Press button B. (The machine will then show Frame 4.)

C. A student will be able to decide for himself when to move to fresh material.

Press button C. (The machine will then show Frame 6.)

FRAME 2 (from frame 1)

YOUR ANSWER : Self-pacing means that every student will be able to get through the programme as quickly or as slowly as he pleases.

You are not quite correct.

Perhaps you had in mind the case of a person reading a conventional book. Reading a book is self-paced in the sense that the reader can get through it as quickly or as slowly as he pleases but a teaching programme entails something more than simply scanning the pages.

Consider the following sentences:

A. You cannot get through a good programme (without cheating) unless you get nearly all the answers right first time.

B. You cannot get through a good programme (without cheating) unless you have understood and learned most of what was intended.

Which is closer to the truth?

If you choose A press button A (for frame 3).

If you choose B press button B (for frame 5).

FRAME 3 (from frame 2)

YOUR ANSWER: You cannot get through a good programme (without cheating) unless you get nearly all the answers right first time.

This is not true because a programme could be written with an error rate which was very low because the questions were all very simple. This need not be a good programme. It need not teach at all.

Press return button and think again. (This will return to frame 2.)

FRAME 4 (from frame 1)

YOUR ANSWER: Self-pacing means that a student will be able to go on to fresh material as soon as he has understood the previous teaching, but not before.

Correct. You have appreciated that the pace which is important is the pace of learning rather than the number of pages per minute or some similar measure of 'progress' through the teaching materials.

End of demonstration sequence.

FRAME 5 (from frame 2)

YOUR ANSWER: You cannot get through a good programme (without cheating) unless you have understood and learned most of what was intended.

Correct. We are agreed that, difficult though it may be, the good programme is the one which keeps on teaching and re-teaching until the student has shown that he understands. The programme which allows a small misunderstanding to develop into a massive confusion is not a good one. We want each student to move on as fast as he can, but not at the price of misunderstanding.

Press button D and check that you have understood what is meant by the Principle of Self-pacing. (This will return to frame 1.)

FRAME 6 (from frame 1)

YOUR ANSWER: Self-pacing means that a student will be able to decide for himself when to move on to fresh material.

Your answer is correct in a sense, although you are being rather optimistic if you mean to imply that a student will necessarily learn best if he decided for himself when to move on to fresh material. If he is honest with himself and sits a mock examination at the end of each section, and then moves on only if his marks are satisfactory, then we have the ideal learning situation. But this is not always easy to arrange. What a programme does is to test

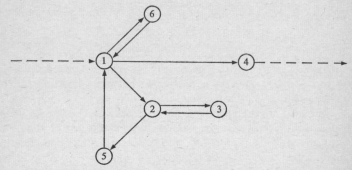

Figure 1. Route plan for this example of a branching sequence

the student frequently so that he knows from moment to moment whether he is understanding and learning. If the programme is a good one, it will arrange for the student to read again parts he has misunderstood or else supply alternative teaching material.

Bearing this point in mind, press return button and clarify your interpretation of the Principle of Self-pacing. (This will return to frame 1.)

Branching sequences can be of varying complexity although certain teaching machines restrict the possibilities. In this example, frame 1 is exceptional in that it does not contain a recapitulation of the previous answer and an indication of its correctness. This would be confusing since this frame can be reached from several other frames. However, the confirmation section can be presented separately to enable the appropriate indication of correctness to be given.

The recapitulation section is intended to consolidate the point by stating how the correct answer should have been selected or how the misunderstanding might have occurred if the choice was a wrong one.

Although historically linear and branching programmes have developed independently, it is important to notice that sequences of both types and hybrid frames and sequences are perfectly feasible in programmed books although not all teaching machines are versatile enough to accommodate mixed linear and branching programmes.

ADAPTIVE TEACHING MACHINES

In our tour of the imaginary classroom we encountered several teaching systems of increasing complexity ranging from the linear programmed book, via branching programmes in machines, to keyboard teaching machines, and finally to a computer-based system which could be designed to embody all the others. Let us consider how far these are examples of adaptive teaching systems.

An animal which is able to adapt itself to changing conditions has a much better chance of survival than one which, although well suited to a certain set of conditions, cannot tolerate changes. Similarly, a device or system can become obsolete if conditions change, or it can survive if it is able to adapt itself quickly enough to the new conditions. This happens in every sphere; a farm-worker's cottage which was adequate when it was built is now condemned unless the owner can 'modernize' it to bring it up to present-day standards of living accommodation. To return to teaching, the style of the textbook of sixty years ago was often a quaint and sometimes beautiful language that never permitted itself one word where a dozen could be used. Such a style is seldom read for information because of its inefficiency as a communication device. We all know that it takes too long to read for the amount we get out of it, though this fact is never supported by measurement. By contrast the teaching programme, whether in book form or on a teaching machine, is evaluated against a criterion test which is used to judge its efficiency in communicating. And if we judge its efficiency we can begin to look for ways of improving it. Thus a programme with its test may be used over and over again without loss of effectiveness so that, should anyone come up with a good idea for improving it, this can be included and its effectiveness assessed by reference to the test results. Any programme which welcomes new ideas because it has within itself the means of judging their worth is able to improve itself as long as its author continues to try them out. And if it so happens that conditions change, if the knowledge and abilities of the students alter, or if the syllabus is revised, or if there appears a new way of teaching something which is clearly worth including, then such a programme with an open-minded author prepared to rewrite it will stand a good chance of adapting itself to the changed conditions. If it succeeds it will survive; if not, it goes on to the scrap heap.

In this way even a linear programmed book is an adaptive teaching system because it learns from successive intakes of students and thereby adapts itself to changing conditions and also improves its efficiency. But this does depend upon somebody revising the text of the programme. With a branching programme there is provision for it to adapt rather crudely to the needs of the student from moment to moment. It asks a question, and then leads the student to a selection of the frames available. In a way, the pressing of the appropriate button assembles a sequence which could be slightly different for each student, since a different pattern of choices will entail a different pattern of frames.

But these simple systems are very limited in adapting themselves to differences between individual students. They can adapt only to gross changes in the intakes of students. The programme remains the same until it is revised, therefore the students all receive essentially the same teaching, although some may omit or select different sections. But let us now take the next step and consider machines which, in a very real sense, compile a different sequence for each student.

In the situations we have discussed so far one is tempted to draw a clear distinction between two components, the programme and the machine. The machine is seen to be a relatively simple presentation device. Even the branching machines have been described as expensive page turners which appear to add little that is essential to the working of the programme. But there are some teaching systems where it is difficult to point to any part and say 'this is machine' or 'this is programme'. An adaptive teaching machine is a case in point. Here we have a machine which continually adjusts its teaching in accordance with the prevailing conditions. Unlike the more rigid pre-programmed machines an adaptive device will compile or select its programme as the teaching proceeds and this will be done in accordance with the student's needs as indicated by his performance to date. Branching machines make some attempt to do this and so may be described as minimally adaptive, but we should prefer to limit the category of adaptive machines to one that is capable of quite advanced decisions for selecting the next item.

There is no point in building expensive machines to do a job which can be done equally well with pencil and paper; machines must justify their existence. To this end various arguments can be offered such as machines bring the teaching situation under more rigorous control by ensuring that the programme is followed in the intended order, cheating is prevented, and so on. The strongest argument for mechanization, however, is the case where the machine is used to carry out some task *which cannot be done without it.* This is very much the case in teaching high-speed skills using teaching strategies of the adaptive kind.

As an example of this kind of situation we may consider the problem of teaching a man to operate a keyboard. He must learn which key or combination of keys to press in response to some given set of signals, say, the letters of the alphabet. He must develop skill at pressing the correct keys immediately he is given a letter and be able to sustain speed and accuracy over long sequences of letters. There are many industrial tasks of this kind, including typing.

Let us avoid at this point discussion of the various possible teaching strategies that might be adopted to facilitate learning of this type of task and assume that we have settled on the following. Practice on each letter-key combination will be given in proportion to its difficulty so that the trainee will achieve an equal skill at dealing with any letter. The keyboard responses for each different letter may vary considerably in difficulty. For example, the letter 'A' might simply mean 'press key number one', whereas the letter 'X' might require keys three and five to be pressed simultaneously. It follows that a different amount of practice is likely to be required on each of these two letters to achieve anything like an equivalent performance level.

When we try to decide on a practice sequence to implement the above strategy we are immediately faced with an almost impossible task. Right-handed and left-handed students will find different letters difficult. Students with the same dominant hand will differ amongst themselves in what they find difficult. Not only this but the same student at different points in training is likely to find that he needs to change the items which most require practice. There would seem then to be a case for devising a system which could structure its practice sequence during the actual course of training. Such a system would need to be continually informed of the state of the trainee's skill in dealing with each of the letters so that it could allocate practice appropriately.

We have chosen this example because we built a teaching machine which, amongst other things, implements this strategy quite successfully. Letters are presented one at a time on a screen and remain until the correct response has been made, whereupon a new letter is immediately presented. A changing letter therefore is an immediate indication to the trainee that his response was correct. Every time a correct response is made the machine notes the time taken by the trainee. From successive response times an average time for all responses is derived and this is continually updated as training proceeds. The machine compares the time for each individual response with the average time, and on this basis decides whether or not a trainee is having difficulty with any particular letter.

The rule adopted by the machine for structuring the practice sequence is simple enough – each time an item is judged easy (the response time was below average) the next letter is selected at random; but each time one is judged difficult (the response time was above average) that same item is reinserted in the sequence. Items which tend to take longer than average will therefore tend to occur more often in the sequence. Several important considerations influencing the speed of learning soon arise, such as how long should be the delay before an item, which a student found difficult, is again presented to him. There are many instances of this kind but enough has been said to illustrate the main point. This kind of strategy cannot be implemented without some form of mechanization. The machine is not called upon to make difficult decisions but it is called upon to make a lot of simple decisions more quickly than a man could possibly make them.

Another device which we might equally well have chosen to illustrate this point is an adaptive keyboard trainer designed by Gordon Pask and known as S.A.K.I.* In this case the teaching strategy involves control of the time allowed for a student to respond to each item and of the amount of cue information (extra help) he is given in accordance with the present state of his skill.

Both these two keyboard machines contain what one could call a special-purpose computer which performs only the calculations required by the system. But in our tour of the classroom

* Self-organizing automated keyboard instructor.

we came upon a general purpose computer that seemed capable of almost anything short of making the tea. The reader may care to pause and ask himself whether this was an example of an adaptive teaching system?

CHAPTER 2

DIFFERENT TEACHING SYSTEMS

FOR the remainder of this book we shall stay closely to programmes and teaching machines, and to the learning of specific material. But we appreciate that many teachers object to programmed instruction because they feel the fundamental aims of education are being ignored. Their views are not necessarily less worthy of consideration just because they themselves do not always agree about these aims. In this chapter, therefore, we wish to consider briefly certain characteristics of teaching situations. We will begin by clarifying what activities we are referring to when we talk about teaching. In conversation the words 'learning' and 'education' occur as frequently as 'teaching' itself, so let us consider briefly the relationship of these terms.

The behaviour of individuals changes through experience of their environment. They behave differently today because of what happened to them yesterday. We call the processes underlying these changes learning, and we distinguish these changes in behaviour from those that are brought about by disease and physical deterioration or maturation. We ascribe to learning only those changes in behaviour that are brought about by experience of the environment.

We shall discuss later how psychologists have made exact studies of learning, as in their conditioning experiments with animals. But all of us are aware of thousands of examples of learning from our personal experience. When we look at some of those simple, everyday happenings we appreciate that learning is not always a voluntary process. It is going on all the time a normal individual moves around in the world, so much so that we might say it is in the nature of man to learn, a basic property of the human organism. This is what the psychologist means when he talks about man being an adaptive system.

Man, then, cannot always opt out and refuse to learn. If a child reaches into a fire to retrieve a ball and gets burnt certain changes will have occurred in the child other than the blisters on its fingers; it will have learned to relate fire to pain in a way that will alter its future behaviour to fires. The child cannot refuse to learn this relationship. Things happen to us and leave their mark on our behaviour, whether we wish it or not.

There is another sense in which learning is not entirely voluntary. We may set out to learn something complex and find that we just cannot grasp it, the concepts evade us somehow. We may keep on trying on the assumption that sooner or later we shall succeed, but we have no guarantee of this. We can muster our intellectual forces, direct our attention and study the subject systematically, but we cannot say we will learn with the same confidence that we can say we will stir our tea or let the cat out.

Now let us look at the more accepted side where an individual chooses to learn. We say that a person can decide to learn French or Chemistry. He can refuse to go to a class, or to concentrate on the work when he gets there. Even if he deliberately does not attend to the work, he may still learn something. He may learn to recognize the teacher or the cover of the class book, and the odd fragments of the subject. But these disconnected items are soon forgotten and progress is minimal compared with the achievements of the same person when he is trying to learn the subject matter. To this extent we say that learning is voluntary in that it requires some effort of the learner before useful learning is likely to occur. What is under voluntary control of course is not the learning process itself but the creation of the conditions under which learning is likely to take place. When a person sets out to learn something he decides to make certain information available to himself, focus his attention on it, relate it to his previous knowledge, try to understand its meaning and implications, and so on. He might be good or bad at this and for this reason he might learn well or not. But we should be clear that he is not able to control the basic processes underlying learning.

To say that the basic learning mechanisms are not under voluntary control is not a philosophy of despair. Both learner and teacher can do much to facilitate learning, particularly in creating situations where learning is likely to occur efficiently. Psychologists have studied learning and the factors influencing it and we shall return to this work in Chapter 3. But here we wish to relate the two subjects of learning and teaching.

Since learning may occur spontaneously when an individual is reacting to his environment any situation is potentially a learning situation. But it will be useful to restrict our description of 'learning situations' to those cases where a set of conditions have been created to enable learning to occur. Learning situations may be created by a student himself when he sets out with a deliberate aim to acquire some knowledge, and does at least some of the things that will make it likely that he will succeed. In some cases they may occur accidentally where events seem to conspire in creating a situation conducive to learning – alas, it is all too rare when we happen on the right material just when we are interested and where there is nothing to distract our attention. But the most obvious learning situation is the one which is carefully contrived, deliberately planned and ubiquitously conducted at enormous cost to the individual and nation – our school system. From time to time we hear howls of rage when some indignant taxpayer wakes up to the fact that the younger generation is learning just as much from life outside school as from inside. There is, of course, no reason why it should not – the more attractive the life outside the harder it will be for the life within school to compete. The learning situation in school is not taking place in a vacuum, but against a background of exciting events created by every possible communication gimmick of our century. The moral is simple enough. What was good enough in the time of Dickens is just not in the running today, and yet we are still prepared to put forty or fifty children in a class with one teacher and a blackboard and expect him to get on with it.

In trying now to relate learning and teaching our position is straightforward. Teaching is the design and implementation of an efficient learning situation, or set of learning situations. It would be neater to say something such as teaching will increase learning efficiency, and we hope it will, but our point is that we do not know enough about learning to be sure what this would mean. So we are content with the clumsier manipulation of the circumstances that bring about learning. Where the learner himself makes the effort to create a situation where he will learn we talk about self-teaching, and in so far as some effort is generally required of the learner there is some element of self-teaching in most situations. But on the other hand a teacher or other external agent can contribute much to increasing the efficiency of a learning situation, and we shall be mainly concerned with considering what can be done and the kind of system that is required to achieve it.

EDUCATION AND TEACHING

Before proceeding with our discussion of teaching systems, let us briefly consider the term that is so much linked with teaching, education. The criticism is often made that some intensive courses forget that education is more than communicating knowledge and skills. We would all accept that an educated man is not synonymous with a well-informed, knowledgeable man. To be educated a man must have knowledge but we expect him to be able to give us more than a parrot-like regurgitation of his learning. We do not imagine he has acquired his opinions by brainwashing and indoctrination but by careful consideration of relevant evidence. His opinions and attitudes if not reasonable should at least be reasoned and certainly his own responsibility.

These ideas are closely related to the educational objectives of our society. Such objectives are not simply a list of things that a man should know or be able to do, or attitudes he should hold. They include such ideas as individuals being encouraged to develop their own interests and attitudes so that the ultimate product is an expression of a unique personality. But this is only within limits. The desire to be a fascist, a morbid interest in pornography, and similar bents which are not compatible with society's ideas of what man should be like, are not fostered but discouraged by our educational system.

Not only are our educational objectives somewhat vague but they also change in detail from time to time and from society to society. It is the special function of our schools and colleges to achieve these objectives, though much is done both for good and bad by mass media such as television, newspapers and popular literature. This places a heavy responsibility on our front-line educators, our teachers, and the task is made especially difficult because many of the attributes that society requires of an educated man cannot be taught in the way that knowledge and skills can be taught within the classroom. It is here that the personal example of the teacher becomes so influential. We have no replacement for the human teacher as an instrument of inspiration or as an example of the behaviour of the educated man. And we have here no direct measure of success. The teacher may hope that he is a significant influence in the formation of the character of his students, but he has little immediate evidence for it. He cannot test this as he can examine the success of his arithmetic lesson. Indeed the final judgement will lie in the future when we find out the kind of people his students become, but even then there will be a host of other influences to take into account. We can see that here it is extremely difficult to discover what educational procedures are effective, and this lack of knowledge of results only serves to add to the difficulty of this part of the teacher's job.

Whereas our educational objectives are stated at a high level of generality and apply to all our students, our teaching objectives can be stated much more explicitly in terms of the things which we expect our students to know or be able to do at any stage of the course. When we discuss a teaching system we will be discussing a system aimed at achieving some specifiable set of teaching objectives, that is, with states of knowledge and with skills, including intellectual skills. Much of a schoolteacher's function is precisely this. This is not to turn a blind eye to the educational objectives we have considered. Many teaching objectives may be aimed at achieving educational objectives but there is a distinction here. If we specify that a boy should be taught religious knowledge or biology our teaching objectives will be specifiable by such phrases as 'He will know . . .' 'He shall be able to . . .' where the blanks will be filled in by statements of principles of religion or biology, theological or biological arguments, what religious men or biologists believe, etc. It is not part of our teaching objectives that the boy should acquire certain feelings or attitudes towards religion or biology, though this may be part of our educational objectives and what in fact we hope to achieve by attaining our teaching objectives.

Now even if the reader feels the distinction between the two objectives is somewhat arbitrary we feel it is useful in discussing the functions of a teaching system. We want on the one hand to state objectives that can both be achieved and be seen to be achieved since so much discussion is vitiated by claims that could never be verified or disproved, and on the other to recognize that these teaching objectives are not necessarily the ultimate criteria of education. These latter are not only more difficult to define but it is well-nigh impossible to say when they have been achieved. Hence the perpetuation of many systems that seem of doubtful merit.

TEACHING AND COMMUNICATION SYSTEMS

We can now proceed to consider teaching from the standpoint of designing and implementing efficient learning situations which will maximize the chances of achieving any specified set of teaching objectives. When we turn to some everyday examples of teaching and see what they have in common we find it useful to consider teaching as a complex example of a communication system. The complexity arises because it is not sufficient for any particular signal to be sent and received; ideally it must be received, understood and retained. Teachers are aware of so many slips along the way – the message that was understood but forgotten, or was too complex and was rote learned without a glimmer of light.

Again the sender of the message is generally the teacher but this single source may be varied and in some instances may be the radio, a tape-recorder, film and so on. This introduces complexities which are further magnified when we realize that the receiver may be one, two or any number of pupils. Teaching is practising the art of communicating at many different levels and as such we should appreciate its complexities. It is helpful to consider models of communication but their main purpose is to illustrate the subtle interactions when we take on the responsibility of not only sending a message to a receiver but expecting him to learn it.

In practice the teacher often finds himself trying to teach not one piece of material but several as he goes over his explanation for the benefit of the slower pupils. How does he know that some of his students have not understood? Partly because he knows his students and their different abilities; partly because he watches them as he talks and can observe their reactions, partly because he gets them to respond, either by written or spoken answers. The teacher has to interact with his class so that his teaching is a two-way communication channel between himself and his pupils. Where the channel becomes blocked at one end, say because the pupils are too timid to ask questions, the teacher may be putting forward a brilliant exposition of his subject but at a totally inappropriate level for his class.

It is partly as a means of overcoming these difficulties that the tutorial system is so highly esteemed. Here, in theory at least, tutor and student discuss together and neither is allowed to hold the floor for too long. The tutor, as the body of knowledge, should be communicating with the student, presumably the body of ignorance, and by their interchange of ideas knowledge if not wisdom is transferred from one to the other. In practice, as any tutor will acknowledge, the exchange is not always so one-sided, but even at its worst it provides the means for each participant to communicate with the other.

It is worth noting how some forms of teaching may represent very different forms of communication. The tutorial system as a two-way interaction between individuals is a closed-loop system in which feedback to the sender (the tutor) is given at every point. Each participant knows when his message has been received and understood, and when not. Knowledge of results is nearly immediate and mistakes may be rectified at once. As soon as we begin to add to the number of students we start to overload the system. It will function with two students; sometimes, and with some subjects, even with four and eight, but it is superhuman skill when it comes to the normal classroom numbers of thirty or more.

The point we have to notice here is that from the standpoint of a communication system, there is often a subtle change in how the teaching is being done. When we are using a film, or listening to a schools' broadcast, or a television series, we appreciate that the pupils cannot interrupt. The lesson will go on whether they can follow or not, even whether they are asleep or awake. Here the teacher accepts he is in an open-ended system; that is, he cannot receive responses from his students. But he thinks this loss is worthwhile because an open-ended system enables him to reach so many more students. This is the characteristic of open-ended systems. In theory there is no limit to the number which can be reached from a single source. The good teacher believes he can compensate for this loss of personal contact by the careful preparation he has given his material. He has tried it out on a sample of students, he has amended it and knows his exposition is as clear as he can make it.

Now the dominant feature of so many present-day communication systems is that they are open-ended. Each decade puts forward technological advances that make it possible to reach wider and bigger audiences from a single source – the responsibility should be awe-inspiring that so many are listening to just one. Any open-ended system places this responsibility upon a speaker but never before today have individuals had the opportunity of addressing quite so many.

In our everyday discussions of teaching we pay lip service to it as if it were always a closed-loop system. But of course it is not. The good teacher is only too well aware of the problem he faces in trying to keep contact with his students. He appreciates that some individuals are neglected and that it is even part of the system that on many occasions students will not learn the results of their responses until several days if not weeks later.

Let us now look at how teaching machine systems fit into this framework. In the first place they have a very different objective from so many current innovations. It is easy enough to perfect devices which will enable a speaker to address a larger group – closed circuit television, overhead projector facilities, and the like. And these have their place, but teaching machines are attempting to put the stress upon individual students in so far as they regard the reaction of the student to the material as an integral part of teaching. It is not that there is any virtue in itself in teaching students individually, but that it enables material to be modified to meet individual needs. This is a big step. At a time when the trend is so much towards open-ended communication systems with even larger groups, teaching machines reverse the emphasis and say the student's responses are all-important and as far as possible material will be presented to accord with these responses. The student is put in the centre of the spotlight. He is not a passive recipient who ought to understand, but the main character on whose responses we accept or reject a programme. It is our experience that this is one of the hardest things for students to appreciate. We say to them 'You are not being tested, the programme is. If you cannot respond correctly it is not your fault but the programme's. It is the programme we shall change if you cannot learn from it.' Students listen to us but so often do not believe us. They have been brought up on a system where the student is always on test, not the teacher. How often at all levels of teaching do we hear the numbers of failures in an examination subject being discussed as an indication of the high standard demanded by the subject, rather than as a pointer to the teaching in the subject being inadequate to meet the standard?

How does the actual teaching system differ from conventional procedures? In any system we have a subject matter store, a means of displaying it, and a student. The subject matter may be on tape, in a book or on film. The display might be on a blackboard, on a screen, or be an auditory presentation as with tape or a lecture. When we link subject matter, display and student together, as in Figure 2, we have a familiar open-ended system. No provision is made for a student responding to his instruction; indeed it may be impossible for him to do so.

What happens when we try to make such provision? Where we allow a student to make a response we must have some means of evaluating it. We may do this in practice by providing him with the correct answer and letting him assess the value of his own responses, or, as in some electrical machines, we may have programmed the machine so that one key when pressed will tell the student he is correct and the others will tell him that he is wrong, why he is, and what he ought to do about it. Thus if we

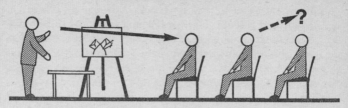

a. With lectures, films, or television presentations, there is no feedback to the teacher. They are open teaching systems

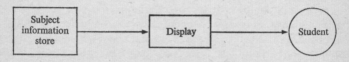

b. Flow of information in an open teaching system

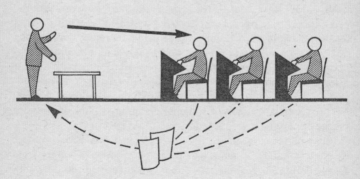

c. With occasional examinations there is some feedback, but it is often too late to help in controlling the learning

Figure 2. Open-ended system

add to our functional diagram a response input and an evaluator we have a system which is now feeding back the student's responses into the machine (Figure 3).

a. With individual tuition or a teaching machine, there is immediate feedback and learning is well under control. Teacher (or machine) and student are in continuous and constructive communication

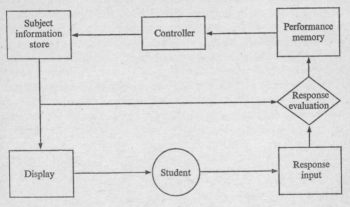

b. Flow of information in a closed teaching system

Figure 3. Closed system

These are the bare bones of a teaching system – we have the subject matter to be taught, some means of presenting this (a display unit) and also of deciding whether a student has received and understood the information. But if this is to be successful we cannot just present the whole of our subject matter at once and expect the student to learn. We need to select the particular information from our subject matter store that will ensure the most effective teaching. Two features in particular will decide this: firstly, the manner in which we have analysed our material and broken it down into steps that interlink with one another; secondly, the state of knowledge of the student, or how far and how well he has progressed in the programme. The system has to be able to store some record however crude of a student's performance. These two functions, a performance store and a controller, close the loop of our functional system. Of all the units the controller is the most important for it is on its decisions that the rate of progress is determined, and modifications to the system are made.

In the future it may well be that the rules governing our controller will vary from those of today. Many of us working in the field expect this to happen. Some educationalists have been suspicious of teaching machines but they need not be for it is one of the basic axioms that such machines must be self-correcting. It has always been one of the tenets that the machine must be capable of learning from its student. If the system is teaching on unproductive lines it should soon be evident and changes will be made. One thing is certain about teaching machines – we may not yet be sure how to teach, but we do know enough to find out when we are wrong. We need not persist in making mistakes.

CHAPTER 3

DIFFERENT FORMS OF PROGRAMMING

In the previous chapter we discussed criteria for teaching at an abstract level; we now intend to examine how far programmed instruction can meet these requirements. We will consider different examples of programming and the nature of their different contributions, beginning with the oldest system, that of Sidney Pressey. As we shall see, ideas about programming have changed rapidly over the last ten years so there is some advantage in following a historical sequence.

SIDNEY PRESSEY

Pressey of Ohio State University is the doyen of teaching machines for he first advocated their use in the 1920s. It was not a healthy time to start mechanizing the classroom, for in spite of the American love of gadgets, the economic crises of the times soon put teachers on the dole and brought in stringent days for education. But Pressey, like a true scientist, had been sharp enough to observe something for which he was not looking. In an era of testing he had tried out a machine for testing students and found that he was teaching them. There is something ironic in this. A corner-stone of our thinking today is that machines are *not* testing students. The student is not on trial, the programme is. The onus does not rest upon the student so much as upon the programmer. Yet Pressey's first machine was a labour-saving device for the scoring of objective-type tests. In American education the practice of using multiple-choice questions has become popular because of the large numbers of students. It lends itself to easy scoring. A student has to select his answer from a number of alternatives, and Pressey designed a simple machine that would score the results for him. The machine pre-scaled a question and the student had to decide which was the correct answer and press the key associated with it. A counter checked up the number of mistakes. But Pressey's machine did not present the next question until the correct key had been found. It was certainly a crude enough method of teaching but Pressey was able to demonstrate that this system of telling a student immediately whether he was right or wrong, and making him continue until he was right, undoubtedly succeeded. It was unfortunate that the time was not ripe for these proposals. They would have been forgotten, but for the violently changed circumstances brought about by world war conditions. Two distinct influences, very different in their approach and yet both having some connexions with the American services, played their part.

BURRHUS F. SKINNER

Skinner of Harvard University built up an international reputation by 1940 for his research on operant conditioning. We should be clear how this differs from classical conditioning as developed by Pavlov.

As everybody knows, Pavlov in his conditioning experiments with dogs rang a bell (the dinner gong), then presented food to the animal and allowed it to eat. The dog began by salivating to the food (the unconditioned stimulus) but soon it salivated when the bell was rung. It was of course important that when the bell was rung the food should follow – the hotel practice of sounding the gong but failing to serve the dinner would not work here.

It will be observed that in classical conditioning the experimenter presents both conditioned stimulus (the bell) and the unconditioned stimulus (the food) and the animal responds to the temporal and spatial contiguity of these events. The animal is not required to perform any response in order to obtain either stimulus, conditioned or unconditioned. Both are brought to it and only then does it respond.

In operant conditioning there is a subtle difference. Action does not begin with a change in the environment but with a response by an organism. For example, in Skinner's experiments on training pigeons to turn around in a circle the pigeon must first make some head turning response before any reward is given. But as soon as there is any suggestion of a head movement the hungry animal is immediately rewarded with food. It soon repeats the response and receives more food. Now it has to keep making bigger and bigger movements in the required direction to obtain the reward until it is eventually turning round in a complete circle. Skinner can achieve this in a few minutes with a pigeon that is at home in laboratory conditions. Similarly he can train two pigeons to play a version of ping-pong by rewarding them each time they knock the ball off the table past their opponent.

Training pigeons by operant conditioning techniques is a long way from education, but Skinner's work had demonstrated how he could quickly establish stable patterns of behaviour. The procedures have had many practical implications, for the prediction of behaviour was sufficiently accurate to make it useful in many situations – for work with drugs, ageing studies, neurosurgery and space research. The essential feature was to reinforce (reward) only the appropriate responses so that the animal's behaviour is shaped in the required direction. But when Skinner turned to the field of education he was astonished to find that so many widespread practices were the opposite of those he would advocate for efficient learning. The teacher addressed not one student but a large class, students listened but did not always understand and had little means of indicating their difficulty, and when eventually they did respond it might often be days before they were informed whether the response was right. To Skinner this was a negation of teaching principles and almost as if it were a conspiracy not to make progress. He set himself to design a procedure that would be as efficient as possible in terms of our existing knowledge from the laboratory. His solution represents the first complete programmed system and is a landmark in our subject.

LINEAR PROGRAMMES

Skinner's solution was certainly novel, but consistent with his laboratory work. He proposed that pupils should be taught individually, proceed at their own pace and receive immediate confirmation that their responses were correct. In order to achieve this he would use a teaching machine to present a linear programme, with the following characteristics:

1. Material is divided into a series of small related steps (named frames).

2. Each frame would give information to a student and require him to make an overt response, usually written. Skinner calls this a constructed response.

3. The steps are sufficiently small for nearly all students to respond correctly.

4. As soon as a student has responded he is given the correct answer.

Skinner wished to use teaching machines because they helped to control the teaching situation. They ensured that frames were presented individually, that students could not move to the next frame without making a response nor be able to see the correct answer until they had given their own, and in general followed the order of frames that the programmer intended. Skinner's argument was that by dividing material into this interlocking sequence of small steps a programme ensured that it was not giving a student an impossibly huge amount of material to digest. The aim was not to lose or baffle a pupil but to explain each step as lucidly as possible, and to ensure that it had been understood by examining the responses that had been given. The student himself would not get lost for he is at once able to check his responses and, for Skinner, this confirmation is a vital step. He claims that when a student has his responses confirmed as being correct this *reinforces* the responses; that is to say it increases the probability of that response being given in the future. For Skinner this reinforcement is analogous to the reinforcement that a hungry animal receives when food is given to it in the operant conditioning experiments. We shall discuss this later, but whether we agree or not with Skinner about reinforcement, it would be acknowledged by all that the procedure of telling a student immediately whether his response is right or wrong is an excellent teaching method.

Teaching machines for use with linear programmes are the simplest of devices for presenting an individual frame and recording a response. Such machines generally consist of a plastic box with a transparent cover over the programme, and require no electrical power as the student himself turns a small handwheel which operates foam rubber rollers to advance the paper feed. As is shown in the diagram (Figure 4) only one frame is visible at a time and there is a corresponding aperture for a student to write in his response. He then advances the programme to the next frame and this automatically advances his response under the perspex cover where it is still visible but cannot be changed. The student can now compare his response with the correct answer and proceed with the next material.

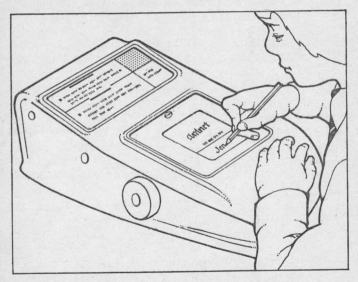

Figure 4. A typical linear teaching machine

A linear programme is, of course, a fixed sequence of frames, so that all students are presented with the same order of material. Skinner contends that individual differences are met by the different rates at which the programme is completed. Provided a programme is suitable for a group of students then the bright will get through it before the dull but both will get there in the end.

BRANCHING PROGRAMMES

Since the linear programme is showing the same sequence of frames to all students it can be presented by a simple machine or in book form. But a different school of thought asked itself whether more use could not be made of students' responses. During the war years the U.S. Services had made use of machines to train technicians how to locate faults in the circuits of electronic equipment – so called 'trouble-shooting'. These technicians had to learn to assess the error characteristics of a problem and diagnose the likely faults from these features. This system was developed in machines such as the Subject Matter Trainer where one item would be presented in a display window and a student had to make one of twenty possible responses to it. The machine might allow him only one response, or give him the correct answer after one choice, or even allow him any number of responses until he was right.

It was a short step to develop this kind of apparatus into a teaching machine. The system of using multi-choice questions is suitable for translating into mechanical terms (as we saw with Pressey), since it restricts the number of possible responses and hence the mechanism has to cater for only this limited number of events. Many fields of psychology such as personality and intelligence testing have used multi-choice questions, but it was due to N. A. Crowder that a further development took place. Crowder argued that instead of throwing away the error response and making the student try again, it should be used as indicating a difficulty. It has not occurred by chance but because a student is misguided in his thinking about the problem. Hence he should have this difficulty explained to him before being asked to make another attempt. This is what Crowder attempts to do in his branching programme. There is more material presented in a frame than in a linear programme and a direct question is asked at the end. The student selects his answer from several possibilities. This is illustrated in Figure 1. To be correct he would select frame 4 rather than frames 2 or 6. In the correct frame he would be told why the answer is correct and then further information would be presented. But if he makes the wrong decision – represented by frames 2 or 6 – he will find there an explanation of why his response is wrong and further explanation is given about the material in the main frame, before he is asked to return to it and make another attempt.

CROWDER'S STANDPOINT

Crowder's position is frankly eclectic. His system is not based on any one theory of learning and his explanation of its success does not lie, as does Skinner's, in reinforcement. Indeed for Crowder the purpose of confirming that a student's response is right or wrong is not to give him knowledge of results but 'to control the behaviour of the teaching machine'. The programme has to 'determine whether the communication was successful in order that correction steps may be taken by the machine if the communication process has failed'. Crowder insists that the system of responses and taking action upon those responses provides the 'feedback control' which he sees as the essential characteristic of branching programmes.

CONDITIONS OF BRANCHING PROGRAMMES

An obvious objection to this form of programming is that multi-choice answers may confuse a student by presenting him with both right and wrong answers. But experimental evidence so far has not supported this case, for students have learned effectively from branching programmes. The reason lies in the nature of the choices that are presented. They are not selected because they are the most likely to baffle a student but because they are useful in diagnosing his possible difficulties, and subsequently providing further explanation of the problem.

The system cannot prevent a student from selecting a right answer for the wrong reason, but even with frames where responses are correct the explanation is restated so that when a student has got there by chance he has a further opportunity to learn. It will be appreciated that the system can only give an explanation to a limited number of choices and to this extent a student is forced into selecting one which may not necessarily be his first choice. To some extent this objection is met by those frames with the alternative choice 'I don't know the answer,' but it calls for honesty on the part of the student to make this selection.

A main virtue of the branching system is that within one programme it tries to meet the abilities of a wider range of students than can be achieved in a linear programme. The exposition need not be broken into quite so many steps and the more able students can cope without making errors, whilst the branching frames can be used for further exposition of difficulties that may be required by weaker students. This does lead us to ask whether the multi-choice question form is ideal for branching programmes or whether the branching could be achieved by other means that might be more suited to the needs of weaker students.

SKIP TECHNIQUES

There is no reason why branching programmes should not use constructed responses or why the system should not be utilized in a more diagnostic manner. If we accept that the aim of a branching system is to take appropriate action on a student's response then we may argue as follows: if a student answers correctly we may confirm his response and carry on with further instruction; if he cannot respond correctly we have failed to communicate satisfactorily with him and we must try again. It may be that this failure is due to any one of several reasons that we are not able to specify in the case of each student. We shall therefore give a further and more simple exposition of the material where we have failed to communicate. This kind of system is known as skip branching and is illustrated in Figure 5. It can be used in a system which allows a student to make a constructed response as well as with the multi-choice answer method. When the student is correct he continues in the main sequence of 'M' frames but if he is wrong he is branched into the sub-sequence of 'R' frames. Any number of frames may be included in the sub-sequence before returning a student to the main sequence. It is in many respects very much like a linear programme within a branching programme.

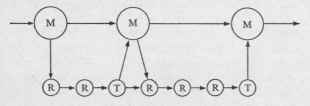

(M) main sequence frame   (R) non-specific remedial frame

(T) test frame containing equivalent problem to previous main sequence frame

Figure 5. Skip branching routes

Similarly this skip technique can be used to carry a student forward. A key frame is prepared and if the student is able to respond correctly he omits a number of following frames where further discussion of this material is given. This is a useful device at the beginning of a programme where students may have different initial abilities in a subject.

PROGRAMMES PRESENTED BY MACHINES AND BOOKS

In Chapter 1 we gave several examples of how programmes are presented, of which the linear programmes in book form is the most popular. As we have seen, machines for linear programmes are simple devices but something more complex is needed for a branching programme. Typical examples of machines that are readily available are the AutoTutor – the example in Chapter 1 – or the GrundyTutor that has similar functions.

A surprising step was taken by Crowder in producing a branching programme in book form – the so-called scrambled books. Here the pages are numbered sequentially but are not read in that order. A student finds that at the end of the frame the alternative answers are denoted by page numbers. Let us say he is reading the frame on page 10; he finds the possible answers refer to pages 13, 16, and 18. He selects the answer he thinks is correct and turns to that page to find out whether he is right or wrong. If he is correct he continues with the material, but if he is wrong the matter is explained to him and he is returned to his original page to try again. This is an ingenious way of controlling a student's progress because it does ensure he reads the material in a prescribed order, but there is no doubt that it is an awkward method of reading a book. Machines have an advantage in presenting branching programmes.

T. F. GILBERT

Before making a critical assessment of linear and branching programmes we should take a brief look at some other suggestions for programming. Gilbert was once a student of Professor Skinner and very clearly operates with almost identical basic principles. But the resulting programmes bear little resemblance to each other. Gilbert's system is called *mathetics* from the Greek 'to learn'. He regards it as a systematic method of planning a course of human learning on the assumption that, since people are at least as capable as animals, they may be expected to learn as well. If we look carefully at the techniques of the animal trainer we should be able to improve on them so as to take advantage of human characteristics.

Animals will learn to do all sorts of things for the sake of a reward such as food. A puppy does not need much teaching in order to learn how to get food from a dish. And after a few successful experiences with a particular dish, he will be delighted by the mere appearance of the dish. Then he will discover that if he wags his tail or barks next to the cupboard where the dish is kept you will sometimes get it out and fill it with food for him. He has learned a *chain* of events which leads to something he wants. Each event becomes valued because it leads to another event which is even more valued because it is closer to the reward. Dog lovers will be able to describe a similar chain of events leading to a walk. The dog will carry out a very complicated routine with perhaps many stages. And you would find it almost impossible to teach the dog this sequence by starting at the beginning, because the early events are of no interest to the dog until he has seen where they lead. Can you now supply a similar chain from the domain of education?

Skinner said that getting the correct answer would be a reward for a student. But Gilbert goes on to infer that frequent experiences of success will diminish the value of simply getting the correct response. What the student is really after, and this is an assumption in Gilbert's system, is the ability to perform the criterion behaviour like a master of the subject. If this is so, what keeps the student working at his exercises must be the knowledge that they are leading to such mastery.

Now the dog has to experience the end of the chain before he will learn the response which produces it. But a human student can be shown the overall pattern of the chain and can learn to describe it before he gets down to mastering the details. Furthermore, the student will accept sub-goals once he has been shown how they lead to the final goal. But in the learning of the sequence of sub-goals, as well as in the mastery of the chains which lead to them, the most motivating sequence of study will often begin at the end. Thus a mathetics programme will usually begin by a very simple overview of the whole course. The first exercise will give the student sufficient instructions and guidance to enable him to describe for himself a very large section of the course ending at the last event. The second exercise will instruct and guide him through the penultimate section but will require him to finish on his own. Other exercises will follow until the student can go right through on his own. If the subject matter does not fall naturally into a sequence of operations, a model problem situation is used as a basis for the teaching.

It is characteristic of mathetics to concentrate on the mastery performance, both for teaching purposes and also for syllabus design. The result is a series of exercises which is designed to develop by guided practice the very behaviour required after the formal teaching has ceased. Thus although the student may first learn to describe the structure of the course in rather general terms, the bulk of his learning will quite clearly be aimed at mastery performance. For unless the student can see how his efforts are leading him to the sort of results he really wants to achieve, he will be reluctant to work sufficiently hard. This is the crux of exercise design. Each exercise must offer the student something he values in return for his effort and attention.

A mathetics programme begins life with a careful study of the mastery performance with a view to describing exactly what a master of the subject will attend to, what he will do, and what he will think or say to himself in order to do it. These three components are then subjected to a most rigorous examination to see if they are the best and most parsimonious set of teaching points. Very often the traditional skills can be shown to be unnecessarily cumbersome or inefficient. Very often the theory taught traditionally so that the student may 'understand' what he is doing can be shown to be redundant or even confusing. Very often the set of tiny fragments of behaviour into which the matheticist analyses the mastery performance can be seen to include a vast amount which the students will know already. All they need is a few new ideas and a new look at some of their old. Mathetics is a system of lesson or programme preparation which is not particularly easy to understand in the initial stages, but it has an astonishing potential which is not appreciated until one starts to apply it. We include it here because in its analysis of the task it goes to the heart of the programme writing; namely, why we wish to include any particular instruction or material in the programme.

R. F. MAGER

By contrast to the methods of Gilbert, which begin with a careful examination of the mastery performances, an approach introduced by Mager starts from a simple demonstration of the mastery performance and then asks the student to call for information and explanation as and when he feels he needs it. This is

Learner-Controlled Instruction. And it is a terrible strain on the instructor. Imagine announcing a title, delivering a brief overview, issuing the examination papers, and then sitting back to await requests from your students. Mager and those who have tried this approach found that the students asked the strangest questions. No matter how carefully the instructor prepared his notes, there were always some questions he could not answer. But after a few sessions on the same area of subject matter, the instructor will begin to see his subject from the student's point of view – often for the first time. He will perhaps discover that his treasured lecture sequences and demonstrations mean nothing to the student whereas a casual aside was providing insight. Sometimes, if he is honest, he may find that he does not completely understand the subject himself! A smooth presentation may conceal ghastly lacunae. But the interested student will soon ferret these out if allowed to control the lesson.

Mager himself used learner-controlled instruction in an industrial training situation and was able to demonstrate the actual job. Each student was allowed to ask for further demonstrations and explanation as often as he wished. This is of course not a particularly efficient type of programmed instruction as such, but in many cases the variety of questions asked and the differences in preferred study sequences will narrow down to a manageable set of 'popular' questions and sequences plus a few unusual questions which are difficult to anticipate. So within this manageable range we might be able to design learning situations where the student has control of the sequence and content. The ideal would be to pre-programme short 'modules' of instruction to deal with all the popular questions, and to have an instructor available for students who could not find what they required in the programmed learning environment. As this instructor discovered new items for the instructional hit parade he could then arrange for them to be made available on request.

But before we all go overboard for learner-controlled instruction, it is necessary to consider what we are asking the student to do. As well as asking him to learn, we expect him to be willing and able to assess his own knowledge and its deficiencies. Now in many cases the student will be perfectly able to assess what he needs to know. And in any case the system tries to supply what the student feels he needs rather than what he in fact needs. But it remains an open question whether the student is always the best controller of the learning environment. Sometimes he will be unable to discern his needs: sometimes he will be unable to ask the questions which will satisfy them. Yet if we bear in mind these reservations, learner-controlled instruction does offer attractive possibilities. It may even be worth our while to train our students specifically for the job of controlling their own learning. And who has not paid at least lip service to the ideal of a self-propelling student who comes out of the educational machine with as much zest for learning as he had when he first encountered it?

DIFFERENCES AND SIMILARITIES BETWEEN PROGRAMMES

So far in this chapter we have spoken of linear and branching systems as if 'never the twain should meet'. And this was the impression given in the very early days of programming by their protagonists who tended to speak mainly of their differences. As we have seen, their origins were in different theoretical assumptions, but the acid test, as always, was not what was claimed but what was achieved. Thus it came about that much research was directed to whether linear programmes were 'better' than branching, and this in turn soon gave rise to a more sophisticated question of the kind 'Better for what? For teaching certain kinds of subjects? For teaching students of certain abilities? The very bright or very dull? The very young or even the old?' And more detailed questions were examined, such as whether constructed responses were more efficient than selecting an answer, whether it was necessary to make a response at all or merely see the answer, and so on. The outcome has been mainly to emphasize that both linear and branching programmes do teach effectively. In very general terms linear programmes are advised where the subject matter is new to all students, or where students are at an elementary level and need a detailed exposition. Branching programmes, particularly with skip sequences, are useful with heterogeneous groups of students or where their background knowledge on a subject is likely to show considerable variation. We shall consider the effectiveness of programme teaching in Chapter 5, but here we will briefly compare the theoretical assumptions of programming.

Most of the psychologists who are not committed in their allegiance to either Skinner or Crowder appreciate that what linear and branching programmes have in common is far more important than their differences. Both systems meet many of the criteria required of any teaching system as formulated by teachers, psychologists, or communication engineers. They represent an active form of learning in which the student provides his own control by reason of his responses. The material has not been written to baffle the student but to keep him climbing step by step, and to be particularly sensitive to those points where he may have difficulty. It is interesting how close the different formulations of the psychologists and the communication engineer are in fact. They use a different language but not always a different meaning. When we come to examine why this should be so certain features stand out. In one sense they are all concerned with the manipulation of spatial and temporal contiguities. For example, conditioning is primarily a demonstration of how the two most important dimensions of our physical world, space and time, influence a biological organism. It is not surprising that they do; for it is hardly conceivable that an adaptive organism (such as man) would not be sensitive to the physical space that surrounds him and the sequence of events that happen to him. But the importance of conditioning studies is that they demonstrate that organisms learn from these related events, as opposed to merely reacting to them. Here it is easy to have the vision of hindsight and declare this was probable enough; yet nevertheless we have in conditioning studies excellent experimental evidence of the circumstances which control learning. Two points are relevant to our discussion.

Conditioning studies do not explain why learning takes place, but they define precisely the circumstances under which it will occur, the variables which will influence behaviour. They are essentially descriptive of behaviour. We cannot say from them why the nervous system, which records and initiates responses in conditioning studies, should be influenced in its learning and retention of those events either by their temporal contiguity or, say, the nature of the events such as the giving of food. Why should two such events as the sound of a bell and the sight of food be associated in some way in the nervous system merely because they happen to occur at the same place and time? And why subsequently, should the food – reinforcement – be so relevant? What is the tie up between the stomach and the brain? Theories have sought an explanation of learning in terms of drive reduction, or the termination of goal-seeking behaviour, but we have no one satisfactory explanation and we have to accept that conditioning studies are primarily useful because of their exact description of behaviour and the powerful predictions that can be made from them. We may not be able to explain learning behaviour but in so many circumstances, as Skinner foresaw, we can say precisely what will happen, and this in no trivial sense.

From the student's standpoint, however, the result is surprisingly clear cut and simple. There may be several different schools of thought but in the main their advice runs on parallel lines. As we have seen, conditioning studies rigorously describe the most advantageous circumstances for learning. On the other hand, the communication engineer is not concerned with learning, but with determining the best conditions for communicating between one source and another. It is perhaps not surprising, but it need not have been the case, that the best conditions for communicating are in fact the best for learning. But so it would seem, for both communication engineer and conditioning experimenter are advocating much the same thing. The communication engineer is equally concerned about the temporal relations of his message. Events must follow events in a particular sequence. He wishes to cut out the distractions from other possibly random sources and in his own jargon is keen that the signal to 'noise' ratio is satisfactory; that is, that the signal he wishes to transmit is sufficiently distinguishable above the random signals in the channel. The conditioning experimenter for his part aims to cut down environmental distractions. Both look for a response from a subject, one in the form of feedback, one for reinforcement, and both stress the significance of temporal contiguity. These are perhaps very simple ideas when compared with the bigger issues debated by educationalists, but in the hurly-burly of the overcrowded classroom they have too often been out of reach.

The different formats and the different pedigrees of linear and branching programmes led to some misunderstanding of their aims and an accentuation of features that are now beginning to appear much less important than was originally thought. For this, early workers had only themselves to blame. They often put the accent in the wrong place and concentrated too much upon the mechanics of the system. Issues such as how many words should make up a frame, whether the response was best made by written answer or pressing a key, whether the multi-choice question was better or worse than the constructed response, were perhaps inevitably to the fore when programmes were first being constructed.

But gradually the emphasis has changed and the accent is now much more upon analysing the material which is being taught, why we want to teach it, what it will achieve, and so on. The contributions of Gilbert and Mayer are typical of these developments and represent what may well be the most permanent contribution of programmed instruction to teaching methods – a critical awareness of its own inadequacies and an effort both to try new methods and assess their results.

CHAPTER 4

HOW TO WRITE A PROGRAMME

THREE PROGRAMMERS

IT is our contention that you do not have to be a genius to write a satisfactory teaching programme, but you do have to go about it systematically and be prepared to amend your effort in the light of evidence. Many professional and amateur teachers have already tried their hand at writing a set of cards or a book which will teach without the intervention of the teacher. And this is essentially what we mean by a programme – a device to control a student's behaviour and help him to learn without the supervision of a teacher.

In many ways the most straightforward type of programmer is the experienced teacher who settles down to capture his teaching skill on paper so that he can reach more students. Since he is familiar with both his material and a few well-tried methods of getting it across to the sort of student he meets in his normal teaching activities, he may begin writing from only a few notes on the topics to be included. But in their permanent record on paper such thoughts may not appear so bright as was expected. It becomes clear that the lesson will have to be amended. And this is what happened to the early programmes, and indeed should be allowed to happen with every part of the teaching process. As the early attempts at writing programmes underwent this revision on the basis of experimental trials with typical students, and even sometimes the more hazardous trial in the hands of a subject-matter expert, so they became more effective. They offered certain advantages over conventional teaching for some purposes, and so a demand was created and our second type of programmer emerged – the professional.

Now the professional programmer cannot be an expert in every topic he may be called upon to programme. Therefore he must cooperate with those who are. He cannot have had experience in teaching all these topics, so he must try to benefit from the wisdom of those who have. In short, the professional programmer must know what questions to ask of the subject matter expert and the teacher, so that he may make up for his lack of familiarity with both the topic and the prospective students. Hence there arose programming systems, which are primarily formal procedures for assembling and classifying subject matter in preparation for programming.

Our third type of programmer has in addition to the problems of the other two the task of conducting research. It would be nice to think that his research was into the learning process itself, but this is a long way off. His research at the moment will probably be concerned with discovering more effective ways of organizing subject matter, and more efficient but still acceptable ways of controlling the behaviour of a student to enable him to learn. A research programmer studies programming systems; he tries to take into consideration the injunctions of the educators, to observe the difficulties of the learner at his task, and the problems of retaining and applying this newly acquired knowledge in the future. And in the end he assembles a series of learning situations which will test some of these hypotheses, or at least, give yet more information about a learner's learning.

When seen from the perspectives of our three programmers, the following account may appear to be too much, just right, or too little, respectively. For the programmer who writes on cards on the top of a bus, it is too elaborate. For the professional programmer it may be just right but so familiar as to be self-evident. For the research programmer thinking in terms of retrieval systems and computers, it certainly misses out too many of the interesting issues. But for those who are none of these it may perhaps give an overview which will be neither frightening in its complexity nor banal in its triviality. We ask the reader's indulgence if some of our examples are somewhat unusual, perhaps even seeming frivolous. That is not our intention. But we write as research workers who are conscious how quickly words mount up in the educational field and how difficult it is to see anything new in such a verbal fog.

THE BASIC PRINCIPLE

If we were to summarize programmed instruction in one principle it would be this: 'Every part of a teaching system is subject to the rule that whatever fails to do its job should be replaced.' This implies that all teaching activities and all its components are but tentative. No matter what the pundits say, no matter what the tradition is, if it does not work, it must go. The same with testing procedures. If students who are ignorant of the topic can still get the correct answer by guessing or other methods, or if those who are experts get the wrong answers because they know too much, then clearly there is something wrong and unfair about the test. For instance, low scores on the test might prompt the programmer to rewrite his programme and make it longer, thinking that his first version had failed to teach whereas the fault was in the test which did not allow for students who knew a little extra, perhaps some subtle point which the programmer had avoided, and therefore answered wrongly according to the marking scheme. On the other hand, high scores might cause the programmer unwarranted satisfaction, because the test was answerable from common knowledge or by guesswork, not because the programme had done an effective teaching job.

Now if all the components of a teaching system must be put to the empirical test, it follows that they must in themselves be reliable. What is effective one day must be just as effective the next. Not more, but certainly not less. This can be difficult in the conventional situation. A teacher may deliver a superb lesson one day which is not due to be repeated until a year later. By then his interests may have altered and perhaps his lesson is not quite so good. More likely, it is better in some respects but worse in others. This is one of the advantages of programming. It may not be particularly effective in the first instance, but it can be made reliable and therefore its faults can be rectified and its successes retained. The same applies to the marking scheme, the instructions for administering the test, and the instructions to the student on how to use the programme.

OBJECTIVES

Teaching costs money. Since we all have to contribute we may reasonably ask to be told what we are getting for our money. We want to know the results of our various teaching systems, and we wish such results to include something in addition to examination marks. And when more pay and facilities are asked for, it is reasonable to ask what it is hoped to achieve.

So it is with a programme. The buyer will want to know what it is supposed to teach, to whom, and under what conditions. Let us suppose you buy yourself a programme on the Micrometer. You will of course make sure it is written in your native language or at least in a language you understand. But you will also want to know what will be taken for granted. You will be disappointed if you have to break off in the middle in order to read up on something the programme assumes you should have known. Again, if you are a slow learner who likes plenty of concrete examples, you will feel cheated if you discover the programme was apparently written for those who enjoy the more abstract realms of pure mathematics. Thus what the programme teaches, and the assumed knowledge and skills of the prospective students, must be determined by the programmer and stated on the cover so that only suitable students will use it. A further part of the problem of matching student and programme is to be sure of the constraints under which the programme was produced and can be used. If it had to be produced on a shoestring it may not teach particularly well but may be correspondingly inexpensive. If you can still learn from it with the television on full blast it may be more useful than if it works only when used privately in silence and without distractions. The professional programmer has now taken to expressing his task in terms of three types of objectives which, taken together, describe what it is he is trying to do. He specifies the *target population* for whom the programme is intended in whatever terms are appropriate. Knowledge, abilities, interests and attitudes may all be part of the target specification, depending on the programme. On the other hand, the actual target population for many of the simple programmes currently on the market is described as 'those who can read and are interested in the subject to be taught'. Similarly, the programmer will often have to work to a fixed budget or produce a programme which will fit in with some existing timetable. Some programmes need to be especially interesting since the students will be required to use them without supervision, perhaps as homework; others may be intended for use in a teaching machine, where the novelty and the difficulty of cheating will perhaps make the programmer's job easier. Such special conditions which might make teaching difficult are specified by the programmer as a list of *constraints*, divided into constraints both at the programme writing stage and on the usage of the programme. These can be seen as objectives which must be taken into consideration when one comes to assess the value of a particular programme in terms of its attainment.

In addition to writing out objectives in terms of target population and constraints, the programmer must say exactly what his programme is intended to teach. This he will express as a set of *teaching objectives*. We have already linked the fact that teaching costs money with the notion that it can be made more efficient when its faults are detected and corrected. And since it has three types of objective, it can be made more efficient in three senses: it can be made to teach better and quicker; its target population can be extended so that more pupils may benefit; or it can be made to cost less or operate under more economical conditions. Constraints and target population are relatively easy to measure and classify, but teaching objectives are not so amenable to objective measurement and assessment. Yet unless the ability of a programme to attain its teaching objectives can be assessed, we cannot be sure that any modifications we make are for the good. Some teachers favour classrooms full of colourful wall-charts, others regard such things as distractions. Only a reliable objective measurement can decide the relative merits of the two approaches. And we need to measure in terms of all our objectives. The charts may attract the students to the classroom and the teacher, but distract them whenever they become less than completely absorbed in the work in hand. A chart of pythagoras theorem may improve examination results but inhibit transfer of the $a^2 = b^2 + c^2$ idea to situations where the result rather than the proof is required.

To summarize, whatever is required of a piece of teaching should be expressed, as far as possible, in measurable terms; as an objective specification of what the student will be expected to be able to do before going through the programme, and what he is expected to be able to do afterwards; the conditions and apparatus he will encounter, and the constraints or special circumstances appertaining to both the production of the teaching materials and to their conditions of use.

CRITERIA

The goal of a teaching system, be it school, class or simple programmed book, is described by this comprehensive specification of target population, teaching objectives and special circumstances and constraints. And to remain economically viable such a system must continue to improve. Therefore we must develop criteria by which we shall detect faults and weaknesses.

Probably the simplest criteria to understand, though not to measure, are the costs of preparing and conducting a piece of teaching. How much to spend on preparation, in both time and money, often depends on the value of the expected outcome. For example, apprentice training is now strongly supported because of the value of trained craftsmen. Art appreciation on the other hand is felt to be valuable, but is much less amenable to 'value engineering'. Nevertheless, in many teaching situations, it is possible to assess the utility of a particular piece of teaching and to allot it a priority which will help to decide what to do if time and facilities are in short supply.

This type of evaluation is reflected by the way the teaching objectives of a teaching system are measured. It is usual to give a criterion test after a programme, and marks are allotted according to an objective marking scheme which is intended to express the relative value of the various parts. Thus questions of crucial importance are allowed more marks than matters of incidental interest. Such a criterion test with its weighted marking scheme is therefore quite a complicated assessment. It can be used to monitor not only the success of the programme in achieving its teaching objectives, but also to some extent the degree to which the programme is coping with the special requirements of the situation.

The third aspect of the goal of a teaching system concerns the target population of students for whom the programme is intended. What are the relevant criteria here? If the annual intake of students is much the same from year to year, it is possible to construct and modify a programme until it is completely successful in attaining its teaching objectives. All the students learn from it all they need to know; the target population objectives and the teaching objectives have all been attained. Needless to say this will not happen often and programmes have to cope with target populations with great variation in abilities and interests. Here it is necessary and usually possible to arrive at a compromise between high criterion scores and wide appeal.

Combining the three types of criteria corresponding to the three types of objectives is an interesting exercise which often focuses educational values very sharply; whether to save money and the time of the brighter students by accepting a certain percentage of relative failures; whether the cost of teaching the very dull or the very bright is justified in terms of the expected outcome; whether struggling to learn or understand is a good thing in itself; whether to teach a subject for its own sake or confine activities to what will be useful and leave the individual to follow his interests elsewhere. But before a programmer can justify writing a programme, or making some modification on the basis of trial results, he must be aware of overall requirements so that his efforts may in all senses be directed to meeting these requirements, in whatever form they are expressed.

STARTING A PROGRAMME

But let us return to the Sunday afternoon programmer with his stack of cards on which he is writing something on the principles of magnetism for Form 5c to use next week if he can manage to get the duplicator to cooperate for a change. What might be his production technique? How does he know what to write on those cards?

If the time is short, the programmer may simply analyse his

material into a list of topics arranged in order and begin writing frames straight away. And he might well produce a good programme. Let us therefore try to follow his line of thinking.

In the back of his mind is a sometimes nebulous image of the body of knowledge which he must impart. If you pressed him, he would be able to describe what his students would have to do to convince a sceptical observer that they had learned what was intended after working through the programme. In a sense, our programmer knows where he is going in terms of what his students must eventually be able to do and what he feels he must teach them in order that they shall be thus transformed from their initial state of ignorance. He has therefore made some implicit assumptions about the starting point of the programme – what the students are expected to know and be able to do before they begin.

Most neophyte programmers find the first few frames very difficult to write. They are prone to come up with a string of 'Mary' frames:

Mary had a little lamb.

What did Mary have?

But every student brings to the programme a vast array of knowledge and skill, some of which will be related in some way to the subject matter of the programme. Since a student already knows something, his first task could be to relate something learned elsewhere to a new idea presented by the first frame of the programme.

Assuming that the programmer has decided to begin by relating something familiar to something new, we must now consider what it is that he is going to try to do with the frames of his programme. Teach. But how? Display information. To an all-absorbing sponge? No, to a distractible student who is not necessarily thirsting for knowledge in that particular sphere. We must hold his attention – and not by demanding an effort of will but by proffering something of interest. And what is more interesting than the chance of accomplishment? So we present a task in which the student is likely to succeed but only after a respectable expenditure of effort. On completion of the task, successfully we hope, the student is to be shown that his effort had produced the desired result, or, if he has made an error, what to do about it.

The first few frames of a programme, when given to those who are relatively unfamiliar with the method, should above all convince a student that this approach moves forward by a series of worth-while steps, for which he will discover he has both the knowledge and the ability. The first thing to teach is that programmed instruction works.

Most programmes to date do in fact require the student to respond to every frame by either making a selection from a list of possible answers or by thinking up one of his own. Thus the student comes to expect some small challenge on every frame. A slow-paced programme will make this challenge minimal and therefore require many frames to teach a topic. A fast programme will ask more of the student by taking bigger steps and is therefore able to cover the same ground in fewer frames.

This is how one of the authors began a programme on how to use the Sine tables:

Sines – Castle's Tables

1 Write your answers in your exercise book or on a sheet of paper on which you have written your name.

2 The table of Natural Sines begins on page ....
   (6)

3 What is printed underneath the word Degrees in the top left-hand corner of page 6?
   (0)

4 What does a little circle like this – 17° – next to the number mean?
   (Degrees. 17° = seventeen degrees)

Here each frame requires the student to do something useful: find the correct page, look at the important cues, show that he understands the conventional sign for degrees. Since this is for a linear programmed book the answers are offered on the back of each frame so the student may check his own as he turns to the next frame. If he has made an error he is supposed to think again and decide what went wrong. In practice, he will seldom bother since the consequences of a single error are negligible. For any important matter there will be a further opportunity for learning the response.

In the sine programme the student is involved by requiring him to arrange his materials and open the tables at the correct page. Another technique for beginning a programme is to open with something of interest which will relate to what the student already knows – but in a novel manner.

1 People who have an income might well have to pay .... tax.

(income)

2 An employer is required by law to deduct .... from an employee's pay each pay-day.

(income tax, also national insurance)

These two frames begin a programming exercise on how the P.A.Y.E. system operates. Notice how the answers are easy yet the vague language of the frames nearly always starts the adult student thinking and worrying about such phrases as 'might well have to'. Although the subject is not particularly interesting, the programme is trying to create interest by its approach. It is direct, informal, and not at all precise. Contrast the corresponding approach of the Board of Inland Revenue:

'Pay as you earn' applies to all employments.

1. The 'pay as you earn' method of deducting income tax from salaries applies to *all income from offices or employments* (except in a few isolated types of cases for which the employers concerned will be given special instructions). Thus 'pay as you earn' applies not only to weekly wages but also to monthly salaries, annual salaries, bonuses, commissions, directors' fees, pensions, and any other income from an office or employment.

Employer's duty to deduct income tax.

2. It is the employer's duty to deduct income tax from the pay of his employees whether or not he has been directed to do so by the Inland Revenue.

A third example of how a programme may begin illustrates the combination of linear and branching techniques for the purpose of forcing the student to think for himself. This section is also trying to foster a particular attitude to learning which must be supported by the instructors concerned.

Your Micrometer *

1 There is an art in using a micrometer. You can learn how to use a micrometer by reading and practice: but to become an expert you must watch experts. If you see one of your instructors using a micrometer, find out why he uses it as he does. Ask questions about everything until you understand it all.

2 Which is the best way to learn to use a micrometer really well?

Read it up in a book	turn to frame 5
Get someone to show you	,, ,, 4
Think it out for yourself	,, ,, 3
I can think of a much better way	,, ,, 6

3 Yes, this is quite a good method. You must be careful, however, to make sure that you have not forgotten something important.

Get an expert to check over your ideas to make sure nothing is wrong.

Go back to frame 2 and think again.

4 Yes, this might be a good idea. It depends on who you get to show you. Even if you asked an expert, he might not tell you everything you needed to know simply because he thought you knew some of it already.

The expert does not know exactly what you want him to teach you.

Return to frame 2 and think about this again.

5 Yes, you can learn to use a micrometer by reading it up in a book. But you would need to get the feel of the instrument. It would be a good idea to have a micrometer beside you as you read.

You would have to practice measuring things and get an expert to check your measurements from time to time.

Return to frame 2 and think about the question again.

6 Excellent. What is your method? Write down a few brief notes to explain it.

When you have finished turn to frame 7.

* B. T. Dodd, Empiric Ltd, 1963.

7 The best way to become an expert with a micrometer is to learn everything you can about it, whenever you get the chance, by reading, by watching, by asking questions, and by trying it yourself.

Turn to frame 8.

8 This programme will get you started. If you don't already know, you will first learn how to read a micrometer. Then you will be given a few hints and tips on how to get the best from your own instrument.

But to become an expert, remember that you must watch experts and learn their art by asking them questions.

Where a student has already used several programmes of instruction written in the same style, the programme can begin straight away on the real subject matter, relying on the student's previously gained confidence in the efficacy of the method:

Production Grinding Practice

1 This programme deals with the piece of equipment that is essential for all grinding operations; the grinding ....

(wheel)

2 The composition of the .... is very important and depends upon the type of material you have to grind.

(grinding wheel)

3 One of the main differences in the .... of a grinding wheel is the type of abrasive from which it is made.

(composition)

On the other hand, if the mechanics of operating the programme are likely to be unfamiliar, the programme must begin by showing the student how it works. This example was written for the Empirical Tutor machine which has three buttons and a place to write down answers.

*Verniers**

1 Write your name on the answer paper – then read the next frame.

2 This is a skip branching programme to teach you about VERNIERS. After each item or frame you may

    A. Skip a few frames

        * B. T. Dodd, Empiric Ltd, 1964.

B. Go to the next frame

R. Reverse back a few frames

Now obey B. (press button B. if on Empirical Tutor).

3 B. means go to the next ....

Write down the missing word.

Always go to the next frame unless given other instructions.
(frame, item)

4 Here's your chance to make a choice;

I understand what to do   A. (to frame 10)

Please explain skip branching in more   B.
detail

5 You chose B. because you want more information about skip branching.

This is a teaching programme which has been carefully designed to help you to learn quickly and accurately how to use .... gauges.

B. (vernier)

6 Every sentence or two you have to do something – make a choice, or find a missing word, or answer a question. Why does a programme like this make you think?

(because you have to answer questions or choose answers every few seconds)

7 If you don't want to learn about verniers please pass this programme on to someone who does. But if you are keen to learn, this .... will help you.

B. (programme)

8 A branching programme is one where you can branch off the main lesson to learn something different. Because this programme lets you skip over parts you already know, it is called a .... programme.

B. (skip branching)

9 You are now at the end of the little branch which explained about skip branching programmes. Reverse through the programme if you want to go over it again.

B. or R.

10 The next frame is where you would have .... to if you had chosen A. earlier on at frame 4.

B. (skipped)

11 Now that you understand how to work this programme we can begin. (Don't forget to write down all your answers.) A small scale which works with a longer scale is called a ....

(vernier)

Having got his programme off to a stimulating or intriguing start, what will the programmer be trying to do over the rest of the programme? The most important consideration is the motivation of the student. Looking from all directions and without respite, the programmer must examine his efforts for ways of making them more compelling. There are books, often paperbacks, which once begun dominate the reader's life until every single page has been digested. If the author of a programme can similarly control the attention and interest of his student, even for the short time it takes to get across a piece of subject matter which can stand on its own, then his task will be the relatively simple one of presenting the subject matter in a suitable form.

Of course, the style of the author will not suit everybody, nor will he be able to maintain interest throughout a long sequence. But the comprehensive criterion test which he gives each student upon completion of the programme will be his safeguard. Although it is difficult to write instructions on how to write a programme, it is easy enough to say how the author will find out his mistakes. If several students fail to grasp the same point, as revealed by their criterion test answers, then either the test question or the programme is at fault. Blame may often be divided equally between the two.

But although the criterion test will show up the teaching deficiencies of the programme, every programmer would like to write a good programme before putting it to the test. There are, therefore, several points which the programmer will bear in mind as he writes his sequence of frames.

When confronted with a large and complicated piece of subject matter to be learned, each student will discover points of interest which he will find it easy to learn, and also matters which are difficult to understand or tiresome to memorize. And each student may experience a different pattern of interests and difficulties. It is therefore essential that a programme proceed through the subject with the utmost clarity and with sufficient repetition to ensure that the required learning, if the motivation is right, shall take place. Thus early parts of the programme will have to be revised and related to the later parts. Ideas learned in a tightly structured sequence will have to be presented again, this time out of sequence so that they may establish an identity separate from their role in the sequence.

And as a student proceeds through the programme he should feel that the pace is pleasantly varied, sometimes slow for a rest and sometimes fast for a challenge. We recorded the cumulative time scores of two students working at the same programme. Student A took 53 minutes, and spent an undue proportion of the time on the last few frames, whereas Student B took 54 minutes and though not as variable as student A, nevertheless changed his rate of working considerably. Clearly, over some sections of the programme both students went at the same rate, but at other places they allotted their time differently. Student A had a post-programme score of 91 per cent and student B scored 79 per cent. Both scored zero before working at the programme.

The two students whose time records were taken both slowed down towards the end. This was expected because the last few frames were test frames in which the student was given a chance to prove to himself that he was up to standard on the contents of the programme. No help was given and the task on each frame could be successfully accomplished by only those pupils who had mastered the contents of the programme. Thus the successful student need have no fear of the criterion test because he had found out his capabilities on the last few frames. The unsuccessful student had the chance to go back in the programme for some extra revision, although we have yet to discover an instance of a student remaining unaware of his deficiencies right up to the final sequence. It is much more usual for a student who is in difficulty to review a few frames as soon as he becomes aware of his problem rather than wait till the end.

These test frames near the end of a programme are designed to effect the weaning of the student from the assistance of the programme and to put him in situations which as closely as possible simulate the actual situations with which he will have to deal.

Sometimes this can be achieved by pencil and paper tests, sometimes the instructor or teacher has to take part. For instance, the Micrometer programme already referred to terminates with a practical test in which an instructor asks the student to use an unfamiliar micrometer to take measurements off a 'job' in the workshop. As he does so, the instructor will observe the student's technique and make notes of any faults in the way he handles the instrument or any mistakes such as failing to clean the 'job' before taking off the measurement. If several students make the same mistake in this practical test, the programme is suspect. The written criterion test is examined to see if these students are failing to learn from the programme or failing to transfer what they have learned from the programme to the practical job.

We have now followed the student from the compelling opening of the programme through a series of small but significant tasks which serve to maintain interest and give practice at whatever will contribute, to the desired final performance. As the programme draws to a close, all help and prompting is withdrawn so as to give the student practice at the test situation itself – not necessarily at the criterion questions themselves, but certainly under similar conditions.

Doubtless, our experienced teacher writing a few frames on a Sunday afternoon will have done all this out of his head or with the aid of a simple teaching plan. But what else would the professional programmer or the research worker do? Let us consider first the professional.

We have identified the professional programmer as one who writes programmes on topics in which he is not an expert. But since his work is expensive and difficult to alter once in the hands of the printer, he must be sure to get his facts right before it is too late. Therefore he must know how to search the sources of information and how to quiz the expert. There is an art in this. Experts sometimes know so much about their subject that they can jump about from topic to topic without realizing that their audience is unable to fill in the missing links. Thus it is that the professional programmer often finds himself asking apparently simple-minded questions in order to get the basic ideas straight before he can begin his programme. It may be that from time to time the professional programmer will take weeks to come up with a teaching sequence that the expert could have written down in an afternoon. But this is not always the case. By the very fact that he must put himself in the position of the ignorant student, the programmer is often given the opportunity to see the subject from a vantage point that is denied the expert because of his more sophisticated knowledge of the subject. Of course, the programmer may see only half the truth and have to jettison his perspective when the expert lets loose the outraged truth.

Let us argue this by what is perhaps an illegitimate appeal to common experience. Teachers will often say that it is not always the honours graduate or the expert craftsman who makes the best teacher. Some do, some don't. But the professional programmer has had the advantage of struggling with many different types of subject matter. He has learned to look for structure and relationship amid the trees of fact and data. And he has developed one or two techniques to assist in this, particularly when the going gets tough and a suitable teaching structure proves elusive.

Probably the simplest, yet perhaps the most powerful of these techniques for discerning the structure of a piece of subject matter or the relationships between the components of a complex skill is the block or flow diagram. Figure 6 shows the P.A.Y.E. system reduced to a few arrows. Yet it shows what you need, what to do with it, and what you get. In this instance it is clear that there are several things to do before you need to operate with the *tax already paid*. Contrast the typical cookery book which leads you step by step up to the crucial operation without warning you that you will require a well-beaten egg-white at a split second's notice.

In this P.A.Y.E. example of a flow diagram, the arrows show where the information has to go and the words describe the operations to be performed and the names and meaning of the resultants. The same technique can be used to show logical or semantic dependence. For instance, if it is necessary to understand A before you can appreciate B, then an arrow would be drawn pointing from A to B: A comes before B. A family tree shows a similar type of relationship structure.

In the case of the family tree and the P.A.Y.E. diagram, the units which are linked together by the arrows are obviously

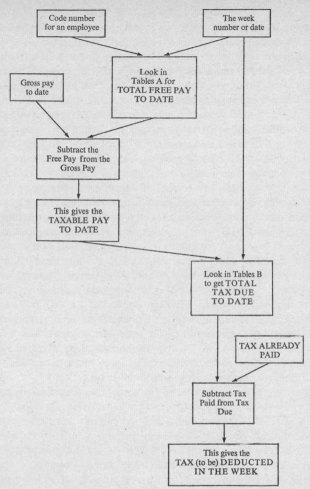

Figure 6. The calculation of P.A.Y.E. deductions

The purpose of these calculations is to find out how much tax should be deducted from a weekly wage packet. The clerk has available two sets of tables (A and B), and for each employee a code number together with the amounts of tax already paid and gross pay to date. The diagram shows the sequence of operations.

distinct. But in many bodies of knowledge there are many ways of differentiating and grouping the parts. For instance, you can study geography by country or continent or by such factors as weather, natural resources, population, terrain, geology. Indeed you can go farther and argue about the relative merits of separate subject domains versus humanities, technologies, sociologies, and similar conglomerates. Here we begin to wander in the realms of curriculum design where passions can run high, but it is important to realize that programmes need not be identified with any particular school of classroom teaching. The programme is merely an efficient instrument for teaching a subject, it need not be identified in any way with any one school of educational thinking.

However, the programmer needs some guidance to explore the subject matter and several systems have been put forward. One is the *ruleg* (rule and example) suggested by Evans *et al.* (1962). The subject matter to be taught is broken down into a set of statements which can be exhaustively classified into two categories called respectively *rules* and *examples*. A rule is classified as a statement of a higher order of generality than an example. Thus what are regarded as rules within one set of statements may be classified as examples in another. For example, 'a micrometer is a gauge operated by a screw' can be regarded as a RULE for which there are examples, but in another context this statement may become a subordinate example of a higher order RULE, such as 'accurate measuring gauges embody a screw'.

The next step is to arrange the rules into a sequence and a Matrix system has been proposed by Thomas *et al.* (1963). One of its virtues is its simplicity and the almost inevitable way it forces the programmer to explore his subject matter. It is not reliable because it depends so much on the judgement of the programmer, and this subjective selection has to be recognized. On the other hand, it does foster communication between programmers, and between programmer and subject-matter expert. We personally favour it for analysing bodies of verbal knowledge because it has been extremely useful both in writing programmes and in the training of programmers. And its procedures are so explicitly formulated that its defects and limitations become apparent long before they have time to lead to any serious waste of time.

In the Matrix system every effort is made to separate the principles and statements of generality from the specific examples which might be used to teach them. 'Men are mortal' is a rule: 'Socrates is mortal' is an example. The rules are then arranged in a plausible teaching order and checked for comprehensiveness by considering whether a student who had mastered the rules would be able to gain full marks on the criterion test. If not, either the test, its marking scheme, or the rule set is faulty. The rule set is also checked to see whether irrelevant or redundant rules have been included. Finally the rules are numbered in sequence.

Let us give the following little story the Matrix treatment:

1 There was a little girl called Mary.
2 Mary had a little lamb (i.e. owned or was borrowing).
3 Its (the lamb's) fleece was white as snow.
4 Everywhere that Mary went.
5 The lamb was sure to go (everywhere . . .).

With a few additions to ensure that each *rule* can stand on its own in case it gets taken out of sequence, we have divided the entire subject matter up into *rules*. Some of these ideas might need examples for teaching purposes, such as 'Everywhere that Mary went'. This could be taught in conjunction with rule 5 by listing some of the places where Mary had been and pointing out that in every case the lamb went along too. This is how these statements are related:

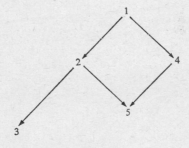

Figure 7

Notice that this flow diagram shows clearly that statement 3 does not make sense without statement 2, and 5 requires both 2 and 4. 'The (i.e. Mary's) lamb was sure to go (everywhere . . .).' Thus the logical starting point is rule 1 and either 4 or 2 may follow. 5 can come after 4 although in conventional language 5 would be more probable before 4 were it not for the fact that this is a well-known poem. Statement 3 is clearly a gross irrelevancy – pure enrichment material.

Thus from the flow diagram which shows the relationships between the *rules* we can prescribe a sequence in which each item is linked to its immediate neighbours: 1, 2, 5, 4. 'There was a girl called Mary who had a little lamb which was sure to go everywhere that she went.'

Although the prose version dispenses with the virtues of the poetry, this example illustrates what we mean by the search for the structure of the subject matter. How it should be taught is another issue and more properly the concern of the experimentally orientated teacher. The flow diagram was in this instance simple enough to reveal the two possible teaching structures. But when the number of necessary rules exceeds about ten it is often difficult to draw a clear diagram since there may be many inter-relationships. The Matrix system deals with sets of rules of any magnitude although it is at its most convenient when they are less than fifty. Several different types of relationship may be plotted although most users advocate only two, association and discrimination. Here is the matrix of Mary's saga:

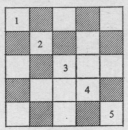

Figure 8

The numbers along the centre diagonal represent the rules. Above that diagonal a hatched square indicates a relationship between the number (rule) on its horizontal left and the number vertically below it. Thus rule 1 is related to rule 2; rule 2 to 3; but rule 1 is also shown as being related to rule 4, and rule 2 to 5. The reverse progress may be carried out below the diagonal, as we have shown in the figure. This not only produces a symmetrical pattern which is easier to recognize, but is also a useful check that relationships have not been missed. In the above matrix the isolation of rule 3 is obvious enough, but the revised sequence shows the characteristic pattern, indicating that each item in the sequence is related to its immediate neighbours:

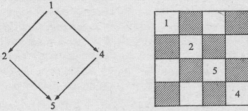

Figure 9

Our experience suggests that the matrix technique is excellent for programmers in training, especially if they are going to begin with verbal material which easily falls into the *rule–example* classification. It is also effective where the subject matter is poorly structured in the source literature, particularly for generating ideas for rearranging the sequence rather than prescribing the order. But the final decision must rest with the programmer. Many matrix patterns have been identified and shown to indicate specific structures, but spurious plots can lead to false interpretations so that the presence of a pattern cannot be taken as a sure indication of a particular structure in the subject matter.

Another approach which has been described by Leith (1964), and which has also been systematized under the rather advanced programming techniques called Mathetics (mentioned in Chapter 4), examines the problem of structure but looks at it from another angle. Ruleg and the matrix systems tend to concentrate the programmer's attention on the structure of the body of knowledge and skills which have to be taught, whereas this approach looks at the learning task facing the student. The method asks of each activity which will be performed by the learner whether it will facilitate or compete with any other activity in the task of learning. Suppose we think of a lesson divided into parts, each consisting of a presentation by the teacher, followed by some activity by the students such as solving a problem or practising a response. Will the first activity in the lesson help or hinder each of the subsequent activities? A programmer taking the learning-task approach will ask himself this double question and record his decision for each part of a proposed lesson.

Then, as far as possible, he will arrange the sequence of parts so that those activities which will be useful preparation for other parts of the lesson will occur near the beginning. And parts which are no help will be placed towards the end. Conversely, parts which can easily be disturbed by the others are presented early in the lesson, and the trouble-making parts are left to the end so that the student can build up a strong image of the correct structure of the lesson.

Naturally these suggestions for ordering parts of a lesson cannot always be followed, and indeed need not be adhered to in cases where the lesson fragment can be vividly presented so that whatever else happens in the lesson it will be firmly retained.

Let us now compare these two approaches. The Matrix arranges the verbal rules in the most plausible sequence so that the subject matter builds up logically. Mathetics arranges so that the learner may do things which will enable him to acquire the necessary knowledge and skills, and ensures that these learning tasks are sequenced to maximize the help they give each other and minimize the confusion and hindrance. Clearly these two prescriptions need not necessarily be in conflict, but they do represent two views on teaching sequences which can lead to radically different lessons or programmes.

So far we have been writing as if programmes were only concerned with learning verbal material. But both intellectual and sensori-motor skills may well be amenable to teaching by programmed instruction. Operator training is one of the most important of the types of teaching in which the syllabus is not mainly verbal. The term *operator* has acquired a specific meaning in this context and is reserved for a trainee whose criterion test consists of a series of situations in which he has to do the right thing and where what constitutes the 'right thing' can be unambiguously described. This usually means that, if the trainee is reasonably intelligent, he could carry out the criterion tasks successfully if there was someone there to tell him what to do. His training is, in a sense, learning to tell himself what to do. By contrast, what we call a sensori-motor skill requires the development of controlled movements of the limbs and often a considerable refinement of the trainee's visual, tactile, and kinaesthetic sensitivity so that he can see, feel with his hands, and 'feel with his muscles' subtle differences that the untrained person is quite unable to detect.

Most jobs of course require some training which is purely verbal – the acquisition of knowledge, some training in knowing what to do and when, and some practice in carrying out the various operations until the requisite speed and precision are obtained. But since these various types of learning may need special types of teaching, we separate them at the teaching system design stage, even though we might wish to combine them later on.

So far the current effort in programmed instruction has been mainly directed to the programming of verbal subject matter and ways of displaying it. And the Matrix technique is a good example of what the professional programmer has found to be a useful strategy for exploring this subject matter prior to programming it. But operator and sensori-motor skill training are amenable to self-correcting teaching methods even though comparatively little has been done in this field. And it should be borne in mind that there exists a considerable body of research on methods of exploring these non-verbal subject matters which will be of the utmost interest when it comes to preparing programmes in these areas.

In order to indicate the sort of analysis that might be used here we will consider a training problem which contains elements of both operator and sensori-motor skills, the navigation of a motor cruiser through a lock.

Let us suppose there is a helmsman and one able-bodied crew.

Both have a certain role to play, and both must be ready to deal with a range of emergencies outside their particular role. They need some skills in their heads, some in their muscles. How are they trained? To begin with, both helmsman and crew usually try to read a few books on the subject. They seek knowledge, and might well acquire it from a programmed text. They will want to know the names and functions of various pieces of machinery, navigational rules, conventional signs and signals on the waterways. At the next level, they will want to put this information into some sort of order so that they can describe tasks as sequences or procedures, very much like the man on the bank who should be able to call out his instructions in the right order but who cannot necessarily carry them out himself. The helmsman will have to be able to say which way to turn the wheel or move the tiller to achieve certain effects. But the fact that he can describe what is required does not mean to say that he will always be able to steer the vessel accurately and without mistakes. Not everyone gets the hang of tiller steering without a period of frantic pumping to and fro, searching for feedback. But with practice, and rarely in the absence of practice, the necessary sensori-motor skills are acquired and the helmsman can make the vessel go where he wants.

But how should one set about training? One way is to unite trainee and boat, cast off, and pray that the trial-and-error method will be effective before any of the errors becomes of regrettable magnitude. It is better for the instructor to go along and 'talk through' the operations, allowing the trainee progressive responsibility. But if the instructor's time is expensive or in short supply, the trainee must be prepared so that he can get maximum benefit from a limited session with the instructor. Thus it is that complex tasks are usually analysed into knowledge and skill components. If the trainee arrives with the knowledge he can proceed rapidly to develop the skills under the instructor's supervision. And the operator skill level is to be found in most tasks: knowing what to do, and when, and how. For instance, how do you steer the boat, or a car, through a gap that is not obviously wide enough? Is this a perceptual skill or can you tell yourself what to do? The answer is a little of both. There is a large component of perceptual skill, but it will not come into full play unless the driver deliberately (at least while learning) looks from side to side of the suspected gap. After a comparatively short history of near misses, scrapes and small bumps, the man in charge will get to know the width of his boat or car and will also get to know what an adequate gap looks like. Then when his eyes start to scan from side to side of the gap he will soon come to a decision of go or no-go. This, then, is a case of beginning by telling the student what to do, and knowing that as he develops the necessary skills he may omit the verbal stages and thereafter execute the operations 'instinctively'.

The same type of analysis will suffice in situations involving several people where each plays a certain role with limited responsibilities and opportunities for action. They can first learn what to do, how to know when to do it, how to recognize when they have finished, who to send information to, etc. Later these functions may become automatic and very much akin to 'skills in the muscles'. Our crew member sitting on the balance beam of the lock waiting for it to fill can be told to save his energies until the water stops moving or the lock gate grunts as the levels equalize. These are the cues for the action of leaning against the balance arm in order to open the gate. He has a definite job to do, a cue when to begin, and another to show him that he has finished. Contrast this well-structured task requiring the very minimum of training with the most untrainable task of disciplining young children. We don't know for sure when to begin, what to do, when to stop, nor whether we have been successful. No wonder teachers, in so far as they are good at keeping discipline, are born and not made! But let us return to the business of writing the frames of the programme. How does a programmer set about preparing his teaching materials? As we have seen a flow chart and matrix will help to indicate the logical structure of his material. But in addition a programmer must explore his subject matter and come to grips with its complexities so that he may guide his students surely through them. Like any other teacher, he will make a teaching plan to ensure that his presentation will cover the essential points in the best order. Perhaps he will make notes of special examples, illustrations and visual aids which might be expected to assist the student. Perhaps he will arrange a sequence to follow the traditional pattern. Perhaps he will essay a lateral approach which is aimed to teach in breadth rather than depth. Some of his sequences will proceed from the known to the unknown, from simple to complex, others will grapple with the intriguing so as to interest the student before taking him through all the details.

And so we come down to the detail of frame-writing. What and for what is a frame? Does that kind of sentence make you boggle? If so, and if it made you think, then it might well be the sort of sentence which should appear in a frame. A frame is a unit of presentation which makes you think or act. A good frame is a presentation which makes you do something which will help you to learn. A bad frame makes you do something which is irrelevant to your learning. It is not always easy to tell a bad frame, particularly if it is out of context. And even frames which seem to be useful may fail because of their position in a sequence. For example, a frame which poses a really searching problem challenging a student may be turned into a simple copying exercise if a similar problem has been demonstrated on the previous frame.

However, there are a few general principles of frame-writing which make sense when applied to all types of programme. For instance, each frame should perform a useful function; it may offer some new information and then ask a question to ascertain whether or not the student has understood the significance of this information. To return to our nursery rhyme for the under-tens:

Frame 8

....
And everywhere that Mary went
The lamb was sure to go.
When Mary had to travel a long way she preferred to ride in a
.... (bus, motor-bike, lorry).
    Ans. lorry

Frame 9

Why?
    Ans. because the lamb could ride too.

These two frames illustrate the principle that a frame should require the student to respond by thinking in a manner which will help him understand, remember and apply whatever he is supposed to be learning. Notice how a new fact is presented not by straightforward display but by making the student choose from a short list using either his common sense or, as here, the knowledge he acquired elsewhere.

Notice also how the frames form a continuous dialogue in which the student is led through the subject matter, not so much by a series of small steps, as by a kind of continuous guidance in the form of short frames which focus his attention on a small part of the subject matter and at the same time prompt him into the thought processes which are most likely to result in learning. We are trying to control what he *looks at* by using small frames, and what he *looks for* by requiring him to make a response. Thus if we wish to make him remember something, we must call for a response which he can supply correctly without looking at something which will give the answer away. He may need some help or prompting to begin with, but such assistance must be gradually faded away so that memory rather than observation comes into play. Similarly, if we want him to think something out, we must eventually test this by calling for a response which will be correct only if he has carried out the correct thought processes.

Now since we have said that one of the functions of the response is to show the student what to look for, it follows that his responses should be correct as often as possible. Yet he will become bored if the programme is too easy. So we must make the programme easy only for those who are working well and learning what is intended. Such a programme will then provide every student with a continuous assessment of his performance. A mistake will be a signal that something has been misunderstood or forgotten. This is why each frame offers a confirmation panel which students refer to whenever they are unsure of their response.

We can now define a programme as a series of presentations of verbal or symbolic materials which has been shown to indicate to the student what has to be studied, how to study it, and also how well he is succeeding.

The rest of the technique of frame-writing stems from the ideas already outlined. Individual programmers have their own styles and ways of dealing with difficult teaching points, and at the present stage of development it is difficult to identify their strengths and weaknesses. The trend is to write programmes which include a variety of sequences according to the subject matter and the preferences of the particular programmer. Our own practice is to write short frames which are sufficiently easy to be understood after a single reading. Multi-choice questions are posed when the student will in any case be familiar with all the possible answers. If we are not sure of the range and variety of feasible wrong answers we ask an open-ended question so that our try-out students have the opportunity to record their interpretations of the question. There are always several. Take Mary's preferred mode of transport, for instance. The 'correct' answer took it for granted that Mary enjoyed the company of her lamb. What if in fact she loathed its persistent following? She might then prefer the bus or even the motor bike as offering an excuse to get away from the creature.

The open-ended question has been called a constructed-response question because it calls upon the student to think out or construct an answer for himself. In particular, programmers following the Skinner model for frame construction will often argue that since a student learns only his own responses, each frame must get him to recall the correct material rather than simply recognize the right answer when he sees it in a list of possibilities offered with a multi-choice question. But you can of course argue that much of life consists of recognizing right answers when we see them and that it is not worth the extra effort to teach people to recall information when all that is necessary is to pick out the correct answer or the relevant information.

If we are thinking in terms of teaching machine presentation it is worth looking at the differences between constructed responses and multi-choice responses. You can tell a machine which answer you choose by pressing a particular button. But the machine cannot read your writing. It might have a typewriter on which you can type your responses, but the cheaper machines have to rely on the student himself to decide whether his answers are correct. He is given the correct answer and must match it with his own and then come to a decision as to whether the match is near enough to count as satisfactory.

It is this very problem of marking constructed responses to open-ended questions that has led to the technique of objective testing. Here there is an almost exclusive use of multi-choice questions for testing purposes because of the ease with which they may be marked. A clerical assistant can do it.

But for teaching purposes, as distinct from testing whether the teaching has been effective, there is not a clear distinction between constructed response and multi-choice questions. If the student can easily think up a small number of possible answers to an open-ended question he may in practice do so, and then consider each in turn just as if the question had been of the multi-choice form in the first place. On the other hand, some multi-choice questions cannot be answered, except by guesswork, without a constructed response. Multi-choice questions in arithmetic may offer a selection of possible answers which all seem equally likely until you have completed the appropriate calculation. In these cases we might say that the student completes a constructed response first and then tries to match his answer with one in the preferred list. Some programmers allow the student the choice that none of the given answers corresponds with his own. This can be called a constructed choice situation and may be deliberately engineered by requiring the student to write down his own answer, perhaps in a way that cannot be subsequently altered such as by writing on a paper tape which is moved beneath a transparent window, and only then presenting the list of possible answers from which a choice must be made.

Another use for a multi-choice question is to limit the selection so as to force the student to take up a particular point of view. And this may be a valuable teaching strategy because the proferred list of possibilities may suggest new approaches to the student. In such cases it may make sense to offer several choices which are correct. This will set up what we regard as the optimum situation for a branching sequence, namely, that something must be said to some of the students which should not be said to all. Thus if choice 'A' indicates that a student has misunderstood, then the programme should rectify this by extra teaching. But if this extra teaching will not take up too much time, and if it will possibly benefit even those who did not choose 'A', then it might as well go into a linear sequence. Of course this extra remedial teaching may be a lengthy sequence in which case it can be reserved for only those who need it. Sometimes it is better to leave well alone if the student has arrived at the correct answer rather than risk confusing him with a discussion of the consequences of choices he did not make.

Thus we see branching as a device for omitting teaching sequences which might confuse or waste the time of those who do not need them. If a group of students really is heterogeneous in its knowledge and skills, then it makes sense to provide a large number of small modular programmes from which a course can be assembled to suit individual needs. But branching programmes have produced a characteristic type of frame which is worth examination, now that we have declared our position regarding its exclusive use to form a branching programme.

The standard branching frame consists of a statement which tells the student whether his choice was correct or not, and, lest he has forgotten what his choice was, repeats it in substance. The frame will then go on to recapitulate the method by which it should have been selected or the reason why it was correct or not. Then comes a paragraph of new material followed by a question for which a list of possible answers is provided. Depending on the type of teaching machine or scrambled book, there will follow instructions to press a certain button or turn to a particular page.

Now linear programmes may of course repeat previous answers and recapitulate how they were obtained, but this is usually not necessary because the linear sequence is designed to elicit a series of thought processes which does not differ very much from student to student. By contrast, a larger frame of the type most often seen in branching programmes will be likely to elicit a great variety of responses, much in the manner of a page of a conventional textbook. The multi-choice question is mainly to determine whether the most important point has been understood, although it can be used to set up a teaching platform from which the next point will be developed.

Having now, we hope, blurred the distinction between linear

and branching frames by arguing that the type of frame is not governed by the type of plan or sequence, we would like to sharpen a different discrimination which cuts across the linear-branching dichotomy. The typical long frame of the branching programme confronts the student with a mass of material which has to be processed in order to answer a question. A linear frame may do the same. Let us call this type of frame an *intrinsic* frame because the exact thought processes carried out by the student are not externally controlled but are governed very largely by the individual student's study skills and familiarity with the subject matter. The programmer takes very little responsibility for ensuring that the student learns what is intended, he merely provides a question which the student can use to tell whether or not his study of the frame has been successful.

Contrast this situation with the type of frame used by Skinner when he is shaping verbal behaviour. He arranges a sequence of frames so that the desired responses have a very high probability of success. He will do this by providing *thematic* prompts which assist the student by leading up to the desired response, perhaps over several frames. He will also use what are called *formal* prompts which assist the student by showing him the form or shape or initial letters of the response words. The type of programme which carries the student along smoothly and without more than an occasional error has been called a *behavioural* sequence because the student acquires new behaviour patterns, almost without realizing it. This is very different from the intrinsic sequence where the student may have to reread each frame several times and even then will get the wrong answer perhaps as often as once in four choices. But now having made this distinction let us blur it by stating that there is obviously a continuum stretching from a sequence suitable for shaping the behaviour of a simple animal to the university situation which has been known to approximate to a single intrinsic frame looking something like this:

Good. You have passed the entrance requirements by working hard while you were at school. Now you are at university to broaden your education. You will have to study topics A, B, and C. Across the quad you will find the library. Find out what the following questions mean, guess what questions will be set in your finals, guess what your examiners will expect as answers, and generally prepare yourself.

Somewhere along this continuum is the optimum for each type of subject matter and each type of student But students are adaptive and will tolerate a wide range. We advocate programmes using both intrinsic and behavioural techniques according to the needs of the teaching situation. By and large, behavioural sequences are good at teaching relatively unchanging knowledges and skills which must be exercised at speed without very much conscious intervention or control. Intrinsic sequences are favoured for stretching mental muscles but must be carefully designed to prevent students wasting time by wandering too far from the point. Short frames usually mean frequent responding which permits close control over errors.

We would now like to summarize the discussion on frame writing by offering a short catalogue of the basic types of frame into which most that we have come across will fit.

Types of frame

1. Information + open-ended question calling for a constructed response.

Example: 'The diagram on the opposite page shows the basic machine tool used in the engineering industry.

What is it?'

This frame asks a question which the student can get right if, and only if, he has understood the frame and looked at the diagram (labelled *lathe*). Notice that this question is not of the form 'What is the basic machine tool?' because that would be a 'Mary frame' (see page 65) which calls for nothing more than the ability to copy.

2. Information + multi-choice question.

Example: 'When learning to change gear you must always follow the same sequence.

When about to change gear from second to third, the first thing to do is:

A Depress the clutch pedal
B Release the accelerator
C Put your hand on the gear lever.'

Here some of the information is not separated from the question because the student will already know that the three items are essential. But not all students will be able to reason out which should come first. Of course this point may have already been made in which case this frame will be much easier. As it stands it might well introduce a branching sequence although one might also argue for a linear sequence since any explanation will benefit everyone.

3. Incomplete statement calling for a constructed response.
Example: 'A Falmouth Quay Punt is a type of ....'
4. Incomplete statement calling for a multi-choice reponse.
'Unlike the punts at Cambridge, a Falmouth Quay Punt .... (can/cannot) put to sea.'
5. Multi-choice alone.

> Example: 'A All intrinsic frames branch
> B All linear frames are behavioural
> C Neither is true
> D Both are true'

Programme size

We have already encountered the problem of assembling a course to suit pupils of widely differing abilities. In practice, the most important differences can be minimized by extra teaching. And this often takes the form of filling in the gaps due to absence or forgetting. It follows that the smaller the teaching units or programmes, the more flexible the system. Each student can have a tailor-made syllabus assembled from standard modules.

More mundane, but often more important are the problems connected with the administration of a course. Lessons have to fit into a timetable. Homework has to fit in with the activities of the audio-visual dictator on the sideboard. And even apprentices are entitled to tea-breaks. Programmed instruction is successful because it can exercise considerable control over the learning activities of the student, but it cannot control his other natural functions. Therefore it must learn to accommodate to their demands. A long programme should be divided into chapters which are as small as the natural subdivisions of the subject matter will allow so that the student may interrupt his studies between sequences rather than in the middle. He may work through several chapters during a study period, but he should be discouraged from stopping in the middle. If this does happen, he should begin next time at the beginning of the chapter. If we are expecting at least some of our students to interrupt their study at the end of a chapter, we can arrange for each chapter to begin with a warm-up sequence designed to refresh the student who has just started again. This sequence will revise any concepts which have been taught previously and which are going to be used later. Towards the end of the chapter there will ideally be a summary in the form of a test which will serve as a reward for the student who is doing well and a caution for the others. When so cautioned the wise student will look again through the chapter lest a thin mist now develop into a serious fog later in the programme. By now we expect the reader to take it for granted that when we say 'test' we imply a test which is marked without delay so that the student can know where he stands before proceeding.

Since the programme is working towards a final criterion test which will convince the sceptical observer of the efficacy of the teaching, these interim tests at the end of each chapter will serve as practice at working under examination conditions, so that when the student is eventually confronted with a formidable criterion test he will realize that he has already practised all the parts separately. This is not to say that we advocate memorizing the answers in order to regurgitate them on demand. What we are more concerned about is the regretfully common case of an able student who gets less credit than he deserves simply because of his poor performance in the unfamiliar and therefore stressful examination situation.

Results

Once a teaching system has specified its goals in the form of a criterion test which allots marks in proportions which reflect these goals, the system will be able to test itself against this measure. The usual procedure is to administer the test before and after using a particular programme and to assess the effectiveness of the programme in attaining its teaching objectives. To begin

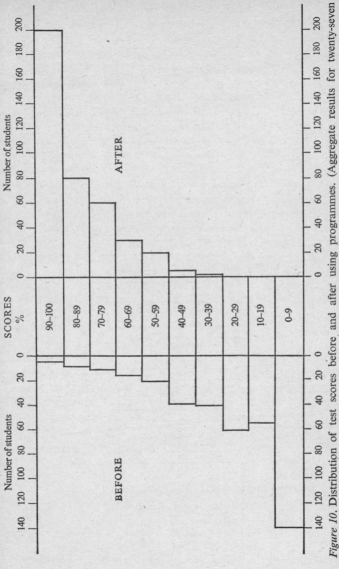

Figure 10. Distribution of test scores before and after using programmes. (Aggregate results for twenty-seven programmes)

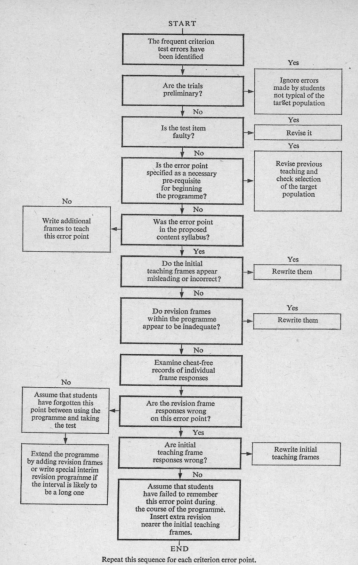

START

The frequent criterion test errors have been identified

Are the trials preliminary? → **Yes** → Ignore errors made by students not typical of the target population

No

Is the test item faulty? → **Yes** → Revise it

No

Yes

Is the error point specified as a necessary pre-requisite for beginning the programme? → Revise previous teaching and check selection of the target population

No

No ← Write additional frames to teach this error point ← Was the error point in the proposed content syllabus?

Yes

Do the initial teaching frames appear misleading or incorrect? → **Yes** → Rewrite them

No

Do revision frames within the programme appear to be inadequate? → **Yes** → Rewrite them

No

Examine cheat-free records of individual frame responses

No ← Assume that students have forgotten this point between using the programme and taking the test ← Are the revision frame responses wrong on this error point?

Extend the programme by adding revision frames or write special interim revision programme if the interval is likely to be a long one

Yes

Are initial teaching frame responses wrong? → Rewrite initial teaching frames

No

Assume that students have failed to remember this error point during the course of the programme. Insert extra revision nearer the initial teaching frames.

END

Repeat this sequence for each criterion error point.

Figure 11. Trouble-shooting logic (or algorithm) for identifying faults in a programme

with, only two or three typical students will suffice to provide the programmer with enough information for a few alterations in his programme. If he is an experienced programmer, his first version may achieve results which justify trials with larger numbers of students. If he has made any serious teaching mistakes, he will want to try out his revised version on a few in order to check up on his revision. Figure 10 shows the results of a year's use of twenty-seven programmes in engineering craft practice. 415 test papers given before using the programme were collected from 118 apprentices, some contributing more than others. 390 papers were collected from apprentices after they had completed the relevant programme. If the before-programme scores were above 66 per cent, the apprentices concerned were allowed to glance through the programme but were not given the test again since they already knew the bulk of the content.

Figure 10 is a composite picture of what happens when teaching is subject to quality control. Some programmes were of course better than others: some had to teach boys who knew some of it already, others had to begin from zero. But from the overall picture we can calculate that all the students ended up with at least 50 per cent correct, and 71 per cent of the test papers were scored at more than 90 per cent.

In this particular application of programmed instruction, the criterion test results were informative enough to permit a revision. But when the programmer cannot identify the faults in his programme from the test results alone, he has to look at the collected responses which the students record whilst using the programme. If several students make the same error the blame must lie with the programme. In practice, the trouble-shooting logic for identifying faults in a programme is quite simple and has been condensed to a series of decisions as given in Figure 11.

It will be obvious enough that this programme revision or trouble-shooting logic must operate under the overriding principle that only essential teaching material, the *must know* category, is worth such rigorous treatment.

CHAPTER 5

HOW EFFECTIVE ARE PROGRAMMES?

ONE of the most significant features of the use of teaching machines is that from the beginning an effort has been made to see 'if they worked' and why. The machines have not been taken on trust as with so many gadgets, and even though teaching itself was the subject its halo of dogma has not rendered it too mysterious to be investigated. Rather there has been a definite effort to examine programmed instruction, to ask what are its aims and why, and whether it is effective; and often as the questions have poured in to us we have wondered why the same questions have not been asked of established teaching methods.

But it is fair enough that the questions should be asked of programmed instruction for the system does claim to be self-correcting. What are the reasons why programmed instruction might be expected to succeed, and conversely to fail?

One point stands out. There is nothing accidental about this success; programming is not an easy way out of a dilemma. It succeeds partly because it tries so hard. It takes its job seriously, it asks what a student should be taught and it has a minimum of preconceived assumptions. Enthusiasm can generally make up for the deficiencies in a method and it could be that early successes were due to this, but enthusiasts soon run out of steam on an exacting exercise such as programming. If programming methods teach, and they do, then it must be because there is something in the method itself. What would this be, apart from the loving care of the individual programmer?

When the main features of the system are listed and shown to good teachers the reaction of many is to say that they themselves do in fact try to teach in this way. It is true that programmed teaching tries to incorporate many widely accepted ideas of learning and teaching. For example, a list would read something like this.

1. Decide exactly what it is you wish to teach. This is no time for generalities. What is it that you wish your students to know or be able to do? Why? Is it an end in itself, or a means for further knowledge?

2. Put the accent upon a student understanding the material.

3. To this end analyse the material into its most logical units. Explain these and explain their relationship.

4. Ensure a student has understood each step as you go along. Do not take this on trust. Get him to make a response so that you can check both his understanding and your exposition.

5. Where he does not follow, accept your responsibility. The programme is wrong and has to be rewritten. This may involve changing a frame, changing many, even changing the whole exposition.

6. As soon as a student has responded he will know at once whether he is correct. Where he is not, action will be taken to ensure that he does not persist in his mistakes.

7. There is no need to put pressure on students. Let them go at their own pace. If they can understand the programme (that is, respond without making too many mistakes) they will learn.

Teaching on such lines is sure to have some success and the query is rather whether we can carry out such a huge task as it demands. It will be noticed that machine instruction has changed the emphasis in the distribution of labour in teaching. Teaching itself, when a teacher actually stands up in front of his class, is hard work, even exhausting, but like any exacting intellectual task it has to be backed by detailed preparation. Programmed instruction is saying that too much effort is having to be put into the actual work of teaching and, perhaps as a consequence, not enough time can be given to preparation and planning. It will reverse the trend by putting far more effort into analysing what it is we should be teaching and how we should be presenting it, and by handing over some of the actual teaching to a machine or programmed text.

The solution is not of course an obvious one. For so long teaching has been regarded as a human task that it is novel to suggest a machine should take over the role of contact with students, and leave the teacher to do the planning and preparation of the lesson. But it does seem to work, and in a world that is short of teachers there is every reason to develop it as far as possible.

Now let us see how programmes do in fact ensure that they are successful.

EVALUATION

We have seen that it is part of the construction of a programme to try it out on a sample of students whilst it is being written. On the basis of their responses, frames are rewritten and any obvious ambiguities are clarified and the level of difficulty of the programme is assessed. In some of our early experiments with programmes in their preliminary stage the programmer sat with a student and presented cards to him. The frame was typed on one side of the card with the correct response on the back so that it could not be seen until the card was turned over. This situation enabled the programmer to watch what the student wrote, to time the frame, and discuss any points when either the student asked a question or the programmer decided that too much time was being spent on a frame without getting the right answer.

This procedure provides plenty of information but it does of course suffer from the disadvantage of putting a student in a stressful situation. The author is watching his every move, ready to pounce on him with probing questions at the slightest sign of hesitation, and all this with a programme in anything but a polished state. Furthermore this kind of exercise needs to be carried out with students representing the full range of the target population, the not-so-good as well as the average and above. For these reasons we have found it better to try new programmes on a teaching machine which allowed written responses without the possibility of cheating. This machine, the Empirical Tutor, also had a reverse button which we allowed the student to use as desired. What surprised us was how much students did reverse when working with a programme in its first version. Unlike the card trials there was no experimenter in attendance and this gave the students greater freedom which they used to look back in the programme, sometimes as far as fifty frames, in order to check on a point they had forgotten rather than risk making a mistake. We gained a lot of information about what was wrong with our programming by studying the points where students had reversed. It was pleasing that as the snags in the programme were brought to light and rectified so the number of hesitations and reversals, along with the errors on the criterion test, decreased. This kind of evaluation enables the programmer to ensure his work is suitable for his students and that he is not sliding over difficulties. But it presents one problem. It tends to highlight the inadequacies of the programme with the results that it leads to many frames being rewritten and to new ones being included. The result is that the finished programme is much longer than the original. This may not necessarily be a bad thing, but a criticism has often been made that programmes are long-winded and apt to be boring. There is something in this – many linear programmes qualify in this category and the tendency to proliferate has to be controlled. It is here that the original specification can be so helpful. Where detailed plans such as a matrix were drawn up, the programmer can examine how many frames he is now devoting to a particular concept compared with what he had originally planned. He can also study whether his amendments have now produced something which is out of proportion to the remainder of his programme. Finally we would point out that it has been our experience that the most helpful procedure is to be optimistic in the initial planning of the programme. Whereas with our first programmes we put the major emphasis upon clarity of exposition at every point, however detailed, we would now plan a much brisker and more vigorous programme that demanded more from the student. If evaluation in fact does show that this is too exacting it will be amended, but because the initial programme was as short as possible the final product falls within acceptable limits.

TEACHING AND I.Q.

Is there any evidence that programmes are more successful with any particular groups of students? It has been said that programmes tend to level the differences in learning capacities among students, in so far as the lower members of the group show the more conspicuous improvements. A moment's reflection will reveal that this is not a surprising result and hardly one upon which we could form any firm conclusions. Most programmes have been written for a definite group of students with some variation in their abilities. The programmer has rightly put the emphasis upon teaching all the group and will have pitched the level of his exposition so that this is possible. Evaluation will have further clarified and simplified the programme. In these circumstances the lower members of the group have the better opportunity of demonstrating a greater gain for two reasons. The amendments to the programme have been more specifically designed for them than say the highest members. It is not sufficiently recognized that evaluation will primarily benefit the weaker students, indeed it could be argued it is aimed at them. Furthermore it is an obvious point when we are considering how much a student has gained from teaching by comparing his final score (after teaching) with his initial score (before teaching), that the student who has the lowest initial score has the best opportunity for improving. Any student who is initially good at the task can show little gain from teaching – he is too near the asymptote of his learning curve for that task. Hence it may not imply much to read that often the lower members show the more spectacular gains.

Two points would follow. Firstly, this is not to say that programmes could not be written specifically for the higher members of a group. Such programmes would presumably move at a brisker pace and present more challenging material. It would be informative to write and examine programmes at this level. To some extent the skip-programme is of this kind. The faster moving main-line sequence is available for the higher student, whilst the slower line has a number of divisions which give a more detailed and slower explanation.

But the second point is more challenging, for it concerns the relationship between teaching and intelligence. In many respects intelligence is a measure of learning ability so that if students are ranked in the order of their intelligence we would expect them to show much the same rank order in a learning test. This would not be so if all the material was far too easy for all of them, in which case they would all have learned the same, say one hundred per cent; nor if all the material was far too difficult in which case they would again all have learned the same, this time nought per cent. Between these limits as the material is adjusted to the students' abilities their learning scores will show much the same rank order as their intelligence. Now what is the task of teaching? To show the same rank order as intelligence? Or to achieve a result where there is no correlation, for example, where all students learn the same amount? In the latter case there is the danger that the brighter are being held back to the level of the not-so-bright. Supposing at the end of a learning session the rank orders for intelligence and amount learned agree, has the teacher taught anything and how do we decide? This is surely much the same order that would have been achieved had the students simply been told to get on with learning the material as best they could. It seems somewhat disappointing if the result of teaching is to produce exactly the same order as would be achieved without it. But the protagonists of teaching say, quite rightly, the order may be the same but the amount that the students know is vastly more than if no teaching had been given and the students had been left to learn on their own. This seems reasonable though the experiments have not been frequently carried out to examine such a fundamental hypothesis.

Are we right to accept that after teaching students will keep the same rank order as in their intelligence scores? Surely, it can be argued, the aim of teaching is to give students opportunities that they would not otherwise have had; that is, to teach them to understand subjects that without teaching they would have failed to understand. This seems a fair point and we have to ask how far can we take such improvement. Will there come a point where with all the will in the world and all the skill in teaching we have to call a halt because the student cannot progress any more? Most teachers would certainly answer yes and in practice long before this point is reached considerations of time and money call a halt to the experiment. But whilst it is true that we cannot produce spectacular results in which students of below average intelligence have been strikingly successful at both mathematics and the classics, we can show many instances where students when taught at a slower pace have learned matter that otherwise seemed beyond their abilities. This of course is Skinner's point. The rate of learning may show individual differences but if it is reasonable to teach the material to a group of students then all will get there in the end if sufficient time is allowed. The point then is that teaching will not be prepared to accept a rigid correlation between intellectual abilities and attainments; rather, it will argue that for many subjects and at many levels of difficulty it will be possible to teach all students to achieve a high degree of success.

The objection to our discussion is that we have failed to say precisely what we mean by our terms. We have deliberately used everyday terms that the layman might use to describe intellectual ability and learning ability. But in fact much recent work has been devoted to trying to sort out the differences between measures of general intellectual ability, creativity and originality. The results are surprising and challenging. In some studies the achievement scores after teaching have correlated little with the mental age of the students, but they have correlated with the originality scores. We would accept that mental age, as measured by standard intelligence tests, does not by any means predict the learning ability of a student over a range of subjects and that several other variables such as originality and personality will have to be considered. It is a fascinating issue of present research to examine these variables and it is to be hoped that in the future I.Q. scores will not be so dominant as they have been in the past. Here our main point is that teaching will not only ensure that students will learn subjects that without teaching they would fail to learn, but that in many instances students who have widely differing abilities will finish with the same degree of understanding of a subject. Teaching does not aim to reproduce the results of nature; it accepts its material – its students – and so often by tapping the whole personality gets a greater response from some than others, with results that completely upset ability tables.

But the programmer who sits down to write a specific programme with a particular school situation in mind will have to have a rough idea of the spread of those abilities that are relevant to his particular programme. He will want to know whether he is to write a programme which will bring all pupils up to a minimum standard, or whether he should aim to retain the differences in individual abilities by making his programme just a little too difficult for some of the class so that the more able people will get higher scores. If he does this, he will of course be able to write a shorter programme and one which need not necessarily hold back the 'high flyers'. But he does run a risk with the others. If he has time, some sort of optional material reserved for those who have time to spare seems to be a workable compromise.

It is customary to refer to the performance of a particular programme by using two percentages. The first refers to numbers of students, the second to criterion test scores. Thus a 90/80 programme has proved that it can be expected to teach at least 90 per cent of students up to a standard of 80 per cent on the criterion test. And remember that it is implied that the criterion test is intended to be so comprehensive that everything of importance has been tested. Those who score 100 per cent know it all: those who score zero know nothing.

To be absolutely rigorous, we would want to know how many marks each pupil scored on the test before he started working at the programme. We have selected three sets of results, Figure 12, which are intended to highlight the quality-control aspect of programme evaluation. Let us be blunt. We are deliberately setting up our programme so as to behave much in the manner of a business organization which takes in certain raw materials and turns out a product of reliable, and preferably high, quality. Our programme takes in students who show by their *before* scores that they do not know very much about the subject. After passing through the 'machine' they emerge with an almost guaranteed attainment level. We can say that since no pupil to date has scored less than say 70 per cent, then we do not expect many students to score less than this in the future, although there is the chance that our initial try-out students were not a representative selection from the population of students for whom the programme is intended. As we have already described in Chapter 4, the procedures for identifying the defects in a programme have been carefully worked out so that should our test results show that some students are not learning well from a programme we can revise it.

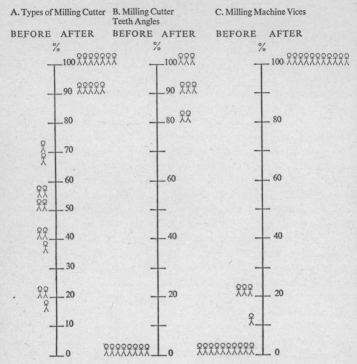

Figure 12. Student results on the appropriate criterion test *before* and *after* using programmes

The three diagrams in Figure 12 show typical results obtained by administering the same criterion test before and again after the students have used the appropriate programme. These programmes were given to a group of pre-apprentices who were working on milling machines. The first programme on the different types of milling machine was very successful in bringing all the group up to maximum scores of 95 and 100 per cent. In this instance, the *before* scores are well distributed over the range 15 to 65 per cent showing that, as you might expect, all these boys knew at least something about milling machines, some more than others. Contrast the second diagram which shows the test results for a programme on milling cutter-teeth angles. None of the group knew enough to gain even a single mark on the test before they used the programme. And even after using the programme, the scores were spread from 77 per cent to the top mark of 100 per cent. This is a good performance for the programme, but we have looked into its defects and expect the results to be even better with the next edition.

The third diagram shows the reverse situation, which is not at all uncommon, where the final scores are all maximum. We do not expect to achieve this over long programmes but it is possible with these short practical studies. The reader may wish to refer back to Figure 10, Chapter 4, showing the combined results of one year's experience with twenty-seven short programmes on Craft Practice. All the scores have been converted to percentages.

THE CONCEPT OF PROGRAMME EFFICIENCY

The perfect programme would obviously enable 100 per cent of the students who use it to obtain 100 per cent on the criterion test even if they knew nothing about the subject to begin with. The little programme on milling machine vices Figure 12 (c) seems to fall into this category although we would want to take a very close look at the test questions and the way they were marked before we accepted these results at face value. But if we assume for the moment that every experimenter who publishes research results is using a reliable criterion test which really does measure how successful his programme has been in teaching what it set out to teach, then it is useful to examine programmes which do not meet the 100/100 ideal.

Suppose you pick up a programmed book on a bookstall which claims a 100/50 performance meaning that every student who uses it gets at least 50 per cent on the test. Is this a good programme? It depends on what you want from a programme. If you are a parent you would be well satisfied if you could rely on the educational system to impart to every pupil at least half of what it set out to teach. But suppose the guarantee was for 90/90. How would you feel if your child were part of that 10 per cent group who get less than 90 per cent, perhaps zero! The point we are trying to make is that performance figures about the effectiveness of a programme are useful in that they can reflect the order of priorities of the author and sponsor of the programme. This order may not be yours, the user. In the industrial setting, it is important to get all trainees up to a certain minimum standard, once they have been placed on the payroll of the company. If the company can afford to sack those who are unsuitable, then its training schemes need not be of the 100 per cent variety with respect to the number of trainees. If the school system has only a limited number of places at the top, it does not have to get its entire intake up to the highest standard; it might well be working to something like a 20/80 criterion. But it would still expect to better a performance standard in the region of 100/20. We would probably not accept a school system which could not impart at least 20 per cent of its curriculum to all its pupils.

But you are still at the book counter holding this programmed book, still not knowing whether it is any good or not. You may have found out that it is good for, say 80/80, and you may be confident that the person who is going to use it is interested enough to be likely to do as well as the try-out students did. What else will you want to know before you can estimate its efficiency as a teaching device? The time it takes the student and its cost. An expensive programme might be worth it if your time is valuable and the programme effective. A cheap programme might be good enough if you are not too concerned with how long it takes and how much you learn. Some programmes take a long time to work through even though they teach well. Can you spare the time? Programmes which are quick to use and teach well are very often just that little bit more expensive because they probably took a great deal of time and effort at the planning and development stages, and they may well contain expensive illustrations. And finally make sure that you do not buy a super fast and effective programme which will teach you something you did not really want to know!

To sum up this section, there are many potential users, such as school headmasters or training managers, who want to select a programme for use throughout their organization and who have to have more than one student in mind. They must think in terms of the characteristics of large groups of students. We will therefore list the details they would ideally like to see in the specification of a programme in order to assess its usefulness. We cannot pretend that all programmes, even our own, always give a full specification. But the following is a fairly typical list and will give the reader some idea of how closely programmed instruction can be made to fit a particular target population of students.

1. *What does the programme aim to teach?* A precise statement of what will be taught.

2. *To whom does it aim to teach it?* The target population of the programme defined in terms of any initial abilities, interests, etc. that are required. If schoolchildren, their age and I.Q. range.

3. *Time:* How long will a student take to complete the programme? – the range of times for different students.

4. *Evaluation:* What is the evidence that it can teach its population? How many of its target population will pass the test? What level of performance will they achieve? What kind of criteria were used in the pre- and post-test? If possible, the actual performance test as set to students. This is one of the best guides to what the programme is trying to teach.

5. *Special considerations:* How the programme was administered. Any recommendations about machines/books: time per day or week: time per session.

CHAPTER 6

HOW TO USE A PROGRAMME

WE have already made the point that the learning process is continuous and not subject to voluntary control. What can be controlled is the environment so that learning in some areas is more probable than others. Taking the view that education is the control of learning situations for the benefit of both the learner and the society which sponsors him and will later and in many different ways rely on him, we must look on school systems as but part of the machinery of education. Some of the other parts may not seem obviously geared to the same ends, but they are. The influence of the home, the disciplinary control of the parents, the value systems demonstrated by the conduct and remarks of visitors and neighbours, the conversation of other children, the conversation of workmates – these are contributing to the education of both children and adults.

In programmed instruction we have seen one way of improving the transfer of information from an individual to another, or from one group to another or from society to its members. Where might programmed instruction fit into the total educational process?

PROGRAMMED BOOKS

Consider first the programmed book. What is it good at? Like all forms of programmed instruction, programmed books are able to offer standardized instruction on a relatively fixed syllabus where each pupil is expected to cover much the same material. If each student is going to require individualized teaching, then the programmed book will probably not be successful. But such cases are few and even then are often due to our lack of knowledge about the differences in learning abilities. So the programmed book is good at presenting the same or similar teaching material to each student. Furthermore, it is able to teach without the supervision of a teacher, or when there is a minimum of supervision this is usually of a non-technical kind such as where an instructor issues materials and marks tests without necessarily being an expert in the subject matter.

Where then might programmed books be useful? Think of a common situation where there can be no supervision by a person qualified in that subject but where 'clerical' assistance is freely available from parent, peer, teacher or instructor. Think of a situation where there can be no assistance of any kind although the atmosphere is conducive to private study. Think of a situation where the will to learn lacks only the guidance of a teacher or expert in the subject. And think of all the many facets of education where learning might be facilitated by just a little preparation – by a programmed book!

At the first level there are the many knowledges required for day-to-day existence: Highway Code; Basic Law; Organization of Social Services and how to use them (including Transport, Telephone, Telegraph, Post Office, Information Bureaux, Citizen's Advice, Police, Emergency Medical, etc.); common emergencies and how to deal with them (including basic First Aid for domestic appliances and cars as well as people). At the next level there are what we call search schemata: ways of looking at and looking for information which maximize the results. In this category of teaching for which the programmed book seems ideal we would place guide books for places of interest and especially for the great storehouses of information such as libraries and museums, and the temporary but specialized sources of information such as exhibitions and 'shows'. Can a programmed book help you find your way round an art gallery? It might be able to help you get the feel of a few paintings and thereby set off an interest that will develop into something more. There are search schemata for some subjects, but we would contend that they had not been subject to the self-correcting principle. If the schema does not in practice lead to the discovery of anything worth-while, then it should be modified. Browsing in libraries or museums is a good way of hitting on a new interest, but how often have you wandered aimlessly down corridors of shelves and cases remembering only the few items which you could recognize or relate to your previous experience or interests? People of wide interests will usually agree that almost anything can become interesting if you go into it deep enough – the trouble and sometimes the boredom is concentrated in the very early stages. Did *you* get past the scales and finger exercises?

Thus we see the programmed book as an individual mentor which specializes in getting across a limited but useful body of knowledge and sometimes a skill which will lead to more advanced learning. We see it especially where supervision is minimal or nonexistent.

One of the faults of the programmed book is just that it is a book. And interest has been known to flag during the reading of non-fiction. Part of the answer is to bring in diagrams and illustrations or even practical work under control of the programme. But much of the paraphernalia of teaching has to be set up by the teacher and many of the things the student must do can be monitored and assessed only by one who knows what to look for. For these reasons, as well as for the more obvious ones, we must fit school programmes into the larger context of the teacher and the society he represents. Thus it is that our present thinking on school programmes is in terms of cheap programmed books, each of which is short and deals with a small unit of the subject, so that the teacher can assemble these modules to suit the needs of the particular student. Short also so that the teacher can make sure that the 'book learning' has been related to practical issues before the student has had time to get lost or lose interest. Since such programmes will have been carefully constructed, they will deal with the core of the subject – the parts that all students will require. This gives the teacher some much needed free time to tailor the periphery of the subject to the individual student, pruning it down for some, enriching for others. Routine learning, note-taking, revision and spaced repetition for the purpose of extended retention can all be handled by programmes and therefore tuned up to optimum efficiency.

TEACHING MACHINES

The teaching machine can, of course, be made to achieve all that the programmed book achieves, albeit at the cost of a higher initial outlay and perhaps maintenance. The book is usually cheaper to publish, but it wears out fairly quickly. Machines that go wrong wear out the teacher. Without going into relative costs which can change radically with the introduction of new techniques, there remain inherent differences in the abilities of teaching machines and programmed books. And one advantage of the teaching machine, which is likely to remain and become more important, is the machine's potential for monitoring high-speed skills. There are a few machines in existence which can assess the performance of the student and make programming decisions many times per second so as to optimize the learning situation for individual students as they develop skills which could not even be monitored by an expert teacher, let alone a programmed book. These adaptive machines are discussed in Chapter 9.

Another potential advantage of the teaching machine over the programmed book is its ability to control subsidiary equipment such as tape-recorders, slide projectors, film loop projectors and working models. In such machines, the programme carries a coded signal in the form of punched holes or opaque patches which are detected by a suitable device and used to trigger off the subsidiary display. Of course, not every student with a teaching machine can be allowed to operate such a device for himself; it depends very much on the student and the level of study he has reached. In our industrial research we have found it convenient to use a teaching machine to collect information that is not available when programmed books are used. Time records have been collected automatically by a teaching machine specially adapted for the purpose. And without special adaptation a cheat-proof machine provides the programmer with a set of responses to each frame without the possibility of their having been altered after the student had seen the correct answer. This sort of feedback is invaluable both in training programmers or when a fault in a programme cannot be located simply by reference to the criterion test papers.

AN INDUSTRIAL TRAINING EXAMPLE

It may seem too easy to speculate on the use of teaching machines so let us now consider a specific example that has been taking place over the last two years. We think of it as a working model of an 'educational' system which has been operating successfully in an industrial setting. Although it is by no means as sophisticated as we would wish, and has had to operate within rather severe economic constraints, we feel it illustrates a self-correcting teaching system in action.

A British engineering company ran an apprentice school which introduced a four-year apprenticeship scheme for the fitting and machining trades beginning in August 1964. The first intake of boys for this scheme took a ninety-day pre-apprenticeship course for which programmed booklets had been written the previous year. The pre-apprentices were then indentured and continued with the normal apprenticeship course which came under the scrutiny of the programmer during the second year of the project.

The core of the pre-apprenticeship course is a set of twenty-seven programmed books covering Fitting, Milling, Turning and Sheet Metal Work. Each book takes between twenty minutes and one hour to complete including the criterion test at the end. An approved marking scheme is provided so that the tests can be marked by clerical staff should an instructor not be available. So far, the scheme has worked as follows: due to the small numbers of any particular type of machine or workplace, there is seldom more than one student at a time working on a particular workshop exercise. This means that, when one exercise is completed, the apprentice will have to be given further instruction before he can proceed with the next. Under the old system, boys often had to wait until there were enough of them for a lecture. Sometimes they would receive a lecture many days before being given the chance to put their new knowledge into practice. Now they are directed to the programme room where they work through the appropriate programme, check their learning by sitting the test, and discuss any criterion test errors with an instructor before proceeding with the practical work. On the sections which have been programmed, the instructors now give no formal lectures and therefore spend all their time in the workshop where they can give individual attention to apprentices who arrive there with a proven mastery of the facts and principles, the calculations and nomenclature which they require in order to get the most out of their time with the instructor. They have no problems of remembering because they go straight away to the practical work where they are shown how to turn their programmed learning into craft skill. What they eventually remember is what they did on the bench, not the words of the programme.

In a practical training exercise of this nature the instructors are able to watch for unsafe practices and poor craftsmanship, the programmer with his collected results is able to watch for failures and difficulties in learning. During the preparation of these programmes the subject matter was analysed into testable sections so that if any teaching failure should appear, the fault could be traced precisely. For instance, a programme on chisel safety taught the apprentices what to do and what to look for in order to protect themselves and others during metal chipping. The criterion test checked that each student knew the facts and what he should do and not do. But only the instructor in the workshop could say whether the book learning had resulted in safe craftsmanship. Thus the instructors and the programmer work as a team. Some of the teaching is the responsibility of the programmer, the rest belongs to the workshop instructors. But when a new programme is being assembled, the instructors suggest the content and supply most of the material. The programmer then gathers it together and checks for completeness and accuracy by consulting with subject matter experts in the company and by referring to the literature. In this particular teaching system, he will then go through the Matrix procedure and write a short linear programme of about sixty frames which the editor will check for style and clarity. When the programme is as good as it can be in the absence of an actual trial, it is prepared for use on the teaching machine (the Empirical Tutor) which collects uncontaminated answers and keeps a time record. When a few students have completed both programme and test, the programmer and editor analyse the results and revise the programme and/or the wording of the test so as to make sure that firstly, the test is comprehensive and fair, and secondly, that the programme gives every apprentice a very good chance to achieve full marks. When the programme has proved that it works in booklet form as well as on the teaching machine it is finally revised again and prepared for publication.

This, then, is how one exemplar of self-correcting teaching practice works in industry. What do the industrialists see as its future? They see first of all the benefits of careful curriculum study which has already streamlined the scheme over and above the benefits of efficient training procedures. They see also increased enthusiasm, not only from the apprentices, who even request programmes without being so directed by an instructor, but also from the instructors themselves who find that they have the time to bring on the slow learner and also to extend the more able boy by advanced exercises which are impossible when the entire group is lock-stepped. Since the instructors are in the scheme from the beginning, it gets down on paper all those hints and tips which make so much difference when it comes to producing a fine job within the time limits which govern the bonus. And since all this wisdom is not only recorded but also embodied in an efficient teaching system, it is impossible for the situation to arise where a master craftsman retires and takes with him a significant proportion of the skill and know-how upon which the company relies.

Programmed instruction provides the industrialist with a chance to take training seriously, just at a time when the Industrial Training Act is giving him every encouragement to do so. Although some of the smaller companies are understandably reluctant to venture into a relatively new field without considerable encouragement they are delighted to be able to buy ready-made programmes to ease their training problems. And for this reason, our cooperative project was directed to the eventual publication of the programmes which might meet a national need, and incidentally carry the ideas into places otherwise inaccessible.

Products and methods of manufacture change so rapidly that the industrialist has problems keeping up to date without even beginning to consider how he can transmit such information to his staff and customers. Although in no sense a panacea, programmed instruction may help here too. The knowledge and skill requirement associated with a new product or method of manufacture can be to a large extent derived at the design stage and during the prototype trials. This is especially true if somebody is on the lookout for it. Thus our ideal self-correcting teaching system in an industrial setting would have very close links with the design staff so that new teaching would be made available as soon as, or better, before a new product appeared. And this teaching, as a programmed package perhaps, would go out to the prospective customers, to the representatives on their journeys from hotel to hotel, and to all levels of management, with suitable editing where necessary.

Think what this means: the innovator will be very much a part of the teaching process whereby his ideas reach their intended destinations. People in design and research are not necessarily good teachers; teachers are not necessarily skilled practitioners. Why not link them to a system which is dedicated to getting the best of both?

UNIVERSITY TEACHING

What of a different level of teaching, say at the universities? Here a rapidly expanding student population has presented a host of teaching problems and this has been accentuated by an almost equally rapid increase in our knowledge in some subject matters. The size of this quite astronomical increase is not always appreciated. For example, the world's literature in a subject, such as chemistry, doubles itself every seven years. Of all the known scientists from the beginning of time ninety-three per cent are alive today. Hence there are no grounds for complacency and sitting back with a neatly tied bundle of lecture notes that will serve for the next twenty years. It has been our lecturing experience in psychology that the bulk of our material comes from studies over the last ten or fifteen years, and that earlier work of the late nineteenth and early twentieth century is being increasingly omitted, simply because there is no longer time to teach it within a three-year course. To find more time we have now had to follow a familiar pattern in other subjects by beginning a graduate school in psychology for students wishing to read for their doctorates.

In such a course it becomes necessary to teach the supporting developments that are now part of the everyday scene of research work. The scientist's specific subject may be psychology but he should be able to programme a computer for himself if he is to make the most of his data. He may wish to run on-line experiments with a computer or design his own equipment so he needs further background knowledge in electronics. Again he should be sophisticated in his use of statistics and so on. Not only is every subject expanding rapidly, but all the time ancillary disciplines are being developed to support any one branch of knowledge.

The trend, then, in so many subjects is to have insufficient time within an undergraduate course to cover the syllabus and to be looking for extra time on postgraduate courses. And within the three-year undergraduate course student numbers have shot up as never before, not only in Britain but all over the world. In such conditions programmed instruction can make tremendous contributions. The picture of the Oxbridge tutor quietly puffing his pipe in his rooms overlooking the college garden as he takes his leisurely tutorial with his single student is so often just a dream. An equally representative picture would be of a frantically busy, underpaid young research student on a government grant, squeezing in an hour's tutorial with two students who are doing the same course which the tutor himself was doing only the year before, and so on. We need to recognize that we are short of good university staff and will go on being short for a long time, whilst in some of the newer countries the need is desperate.

An obvious contribution that programmes could make now is towards good initial courses that are so necessary if students are to get started on university studies. The consequence of drawing upon a wider university student population is for it to have considerably more diversity in its background knowledge. But often in some subjects a university teacher cannot begin the 'meat' of his course without presupposing certain knowledge. When he finds his students have not got this information he has to waste a lot of everybody's time in term giving it to them. This is no fault of the students and it is often essential that this early material is well taught and thoroughly comprehended. University chemists in particular have suffered from their students being insufficiently prepared for their studies and have begun writing programmes to meet this need.

Another area for the use of programmes is where students are required to know some new subject that hitherto has not been within their field of study. For example, many students at university are reading subjects in the social sciences when they have specialized in arts subjects at school. We will not comment on the general absurdity of our educational system that encourages this type of early specialization but it results in students coming to the university with minimum requirements in mathematics and none at all in the biological sciences and statistics. Yet such students need to acquire a sophisticated use of statistics and have nearly forgotten how to use logarithm tables. In these circumstances programmed instruction can be most helpful. With a subject such as statistics it can provide a necessary background and introduce students to basic concepts. It is our teaching experience that statistics can be an off-putting, if not frightening subject for many girl students who have an arts background, and who often have been taught mathematics in the junior forms in an appalling fashion. Programming can do much to get them started and overcome their initial doubts about their statistical abilities. It is the advantage of such programmes that they are always available and a student can repeat them if he feels unsure of his knowledge.

A third area would be in teaching specialized courses which relatively few students would be taking at any one time. Here the programme is used to supplement the teaching staff, who might have the necessary background knowledge in the subject but not the particular speciality that is required. As the number of such special subjects is continuously growing it is not always possible for every university to have experts in such fields and this form of teaching should increase.

TEACHER WITH PROGRAMMES, NOT TEACHER VERSUS PROGRAMME

Our last examples have involved the teacher in using a programme to supplement regular instruction and this again raises the question how programmes may best be employed. It may be that in some circumstances there is no option and the programme has to operate without a teacher because none is available. But in many instances there may be a choice as to how far a teacher will employ programmed instruction. The Royal Navy has carried out several studies on the value of programmed instruction and one is particularly enlightening on this point. A teaching machine programme had been used in one experiment which covered a four-week electronics course for radio and electrical mechanics. This programme was known to teach naval ratings satisfactorily when tested on its own, and now it was employed in an experiment with three matched groups of naval personnel. One group was taught under a condition called Automated Programmed Instruction in which theoretical instruction was wholly on teaching machines. A second, Normal Instruction, received its theoretical teaching from an instructor in the usual way. For the third group, Integrated Programmed Instruction, tutorial periods with the instructor supplemented the machine sessions. All groups had laboratory classes. For the 'integrated' programmed instruction group it was thought that the hundred-odd hours of the course should be divided as follows:

	Times	
	Estimated	*Experiment*
Programmed Instruction	40 hrs	42 hrs
Laboratory Classes	40 ,,	30 ,,
Class Tutorials	20 ,,	28 ,,

Practical factors made it necessary to amend the estimated times and the actual hours for the experiment are given by the figures in the experimental column.

All groups spent the same total number of hours on the course but the aim was to compare how two tried methods, namely a normal instructor course of four weeks and a tested programme of 1,187 frames would compare with a new method which aimed to combine some of the features of each. In the integrated group the tutorial sessions took place in a classroom but instruction was more informal than is possible in lecture periods. The instructing officer used these sessions for discussions of difficulties, revision of main topics, and in any way that he judged fit in the light of how his class was responding to the machine instruction.

Results were challengingly clear cut. On both examination results and laboratory marks the integrated programmed instruction group was superior to the normally instructed and machine instructed groups. This might have been expected, but this was achieved with the one instructor looking after twice as many students in the integrated group as in either of the other two. Both student and instructor attitudes were favourable to this integrated system. On the other hand, the normally instructed group did better than the 'machine only' group.

The Navy has had considerable experience in these types of experiment and their ratings are not likely to suffer from any undue enthusiasm for educational research. We can rely on their findings not presenting a glamourized picture and it would seem that we have here an important suggestion for future developments in the use of programmed instruction. Where it is possible to supplement it with a normal teacher we may have a powerful teaching procedure, for the programme can lighten the teacher's role by presenting much detailed exposition, and the teacher can then give his time to sorting out the difficulties of individual students and devoting that attention to them that would be impossible in normal conditions. We are always trying to make a precious but limited supply of teachers go a long way – here is one suggestion how it may go a little farther.

CHAPTER 7

RESEARCH PROBLEMS WITH TEACHING MACHINES

RESEARCH in this field has had many aims and has gradually become more sophisticated. There was a need for this for much of the earlier work took only the obvious step of comparing machines and human teachers. As so often the obvious step does not get very far. These comparisons of man versus machine were challenging stuff and good ammunition for a debate, but the findings need to be examined with suspicion. Since, however, the machine-teacher comparison has been so popular, and is still the most frequent question that the layman asks of the programmer, it is worth discussing the findings and indicating the kinds of problems in this area.

THE COMPARISON EXPERIMENT: TEACHING MACHINE VERSUS HUMAN TEACHER

The paradigm experiment in science is to compare two conditions A and B where as far as possible the two situations differ in only one respect. For instance, in an experiment on drugs, a group of forty volunteers is divided into two equal groups by tossing a coin. Group A is given a pill containing the drug, group B receives an identical pill – a placebo – which looks and tastes the same but which does not contain the drug. None of the volunteers knows whether he has taken the drug or the placebo. Then both groups are studied to see if the behaviour (physical, chemical or psychological) of group A differs from that of group B. (In the best-controlled experiments the experimenter does not even know which groups have taken drug and placebo until after the results are analysed.) The comparable experiment in teaching is to divide a class into two matched groups or use two comparable classes, and teach class A by one method and class B by another. For instance, class A might learn from teaching machines and class B by their normal classroom methods. Both classes will sit the same examination at the end of each teaching session and the results will be reported in the form of comparisons between methods, and between classes. Subsequently group B might have a session on the teaching machine while A has normal classroom teaching, and the interaction is examined. When there are differences they will appear in the form that, for instance, teaching machines taught as well as the normal teacher but took less time, or, the pupils learned equally well from both methods but preferred the classroom teacher to the machines.

Whatever the outcome of such a comparative experiment, we should ask what conclusions may legitimately be drawn from it? If one programme and one teacher take part we shall be able to say only that, for instance, the particular programmer was as successful using the medium of programmed instruction as was that particular teacher using the medium of conventional teaching. And furthermore, whereas the programme can be inspected after the experiment is over, the activities of the classroom teacher cannot be analysed. This is clearly not a very useful experimental result.

But as an isolated experiment that is all we are entitled to conclude. It tells us little enough about the relative merits of programmes and teachers in general, for either representative may be particularly good or bad and so account for the result. To some extent this chance element in sampling may be controlled where instead of one teacher and one programme we may have the results from very many experiments. Here we are on safer ground. In fact this comparison type of study has been made many times and in a substantial majority of cases programmed instruction has produced better results (we will try later to say what is meant by 'better' in this context). Even here, however, caution is needed in interpreting these favourable results for programmes. The situations are not as simple as they seem at first sight, and we will consider a few of the variables that need to be controlled in such experiments.

NOVELTY

A human teacher is a well-established member of the species, but a teaching machine is relatively new. Indeed, it has been claimed that the machine works because of its novelty. There may be something in this. It is nearly always true that students are receiving much more instruction from human teachers than from machines, so that programmed instruction has the advantage of providing a break in normal teaching routine.

But it is generally true that students are not sophisticated in their use of machines. It has been our experience that students have to learn how to get the best out of programmed instruction. Traditional teaching methods are too close to testing procedures to produce a good transfer to the machine situation, with the result that students are, at first, much too suspicious. But many of our students encounter several programmes in various stages of development, some in a teaching machine, most as programmed books. We strongly suspect that they learn how to use programmes because they discover that they are effective teaching instruments. With repeated experiences of successful learning we hope the temptation not to follow instructions will decrease. We are certain that this can take place from our experience with engineering apprentices. In the early stages of the project we wrote programmes that progressed slowly and carefully with ample repetition so that even the slowest student could understand and learn. Today these early programmes seem dull and pedantic. We now think our students can take faster-moving programmes. Having demonstrated to them that using programmes in the proper manner does teach successfully, we are able to exercise a surprising degree of control over their learning behaviour. From our experiences we conclude that experiments with teaching methods should ensure adequate 'warm-up'. It is worth considerable effort to convert the students and engage their interest and cooperation.

SOCIAL AND GROUP INFLUENCES

It is unfortunate that most research into teaching cannot be disguised from the pupils, so that any experimenter needs to be wary of the effects that discipline and other forms of persuasion have upon results. It does not make for reliable findings when experiments are conducted in the dinner hour with compulsory attendance. Nor, on the other hand, when the experimenter descends from the university with suitable aplomb to carry out a study with the headmaster taking a personal interest. Here he returns with a fine set of results which confirm either his own expectations or the headmaster's depending on who has the more impressive personality for the students.

It may seem unnecessary to mention social and group influences since instruction is on an individual basis. But many experiments have been with well-structured groups such as a workshop or school class, and pupils do not shed their group role immediately on being given an individual programme. For instance, a group leader by some remark may easily set a whole class for or against the method or experimenter. Again, students often like to work together. Now this is impossible if the students are given different programmes, but even so the pace of one student's responses has been shown to influence the pace of another's. One will hang back in order to be responding to frames at the same rate as another, despite working on different materials. Sometimes the fast learners are reluctant to show themselves up by finishing before the others, and we all know the familiar case of the student who must finish first regardless of how many mistakes he makes.

It has been our experience that group influences on individual student's results have often played a much larger part in experiments than has been suspected, quite apart from the obvious point that pupils will always try to help one another. The experimenter has to watch that he is not marking a group exercise.

When selecting students for experiments it is not easy to ensure that groups are as identical as possible. We do not compare the efficiency of teaching method A with method B by giving A to a group of volunteers and B to the remainder: or A to a group just before lunch and B just after; or A to our own class and B to someone else's. Again, we do not give method A to the boys and B to the girls. The little evidence we have indicating different results by the sexes with these methods suggests that the girls tend to make fewer errors and are more conscientious than the boys when working with programmes in book form.

THE LENGTH OF PROGRAMMES IN EXPERIMENTS

A basic criticism is that too many experiments compare teaching situations when using extremely short programmes. Such efforts hardly represent sustained efforts at teaching and are particularly vulnerable to chance influences that may arise in giving the programme. It was inevitable that in the early days of machines we should have a proliferation of short programmes since they are relatively inexpensive to produce and programmers are keen to try out their efforts. But no great weight should ever be placed on a comparison based on a single lesson. Fortunately, results of short and long programmes have not shown marked differences and there are reliable examples of satisfactory teaching with long programmes involving lessons over a term and a year.

CRITERIA FOR TESTING A PROGRAMME

With so many variables influencing the results of comparison experiments it is important that research should set up more refined measures for gauging the effects of its teaching. What precisely is meant by saying one method is better than another? Or is it the old case of better for what?

Programmes have been written with clearly defined aims and to this extent criteria can be set up to see how far they meet their intentions. An obvious measure, one that need not always agree with a measure of learning, is the number of frames where responses are correct and where they are not. This measure will quickly tell a programmer something about his programme – whether students are finding it too easy and getting everything correct or too difficult and making many mistakes. Or it may be that the programme in general is at the right level of difficulty but certain frames require attention since nearly everybody makes a mistake on them. It is here that it is most useful to have as much information as possible, and for this reason we have had students work through programmes on a teaching machine which was coupled to a recording device giving the times for each response. The machine ensured that students were not taking a look at the answer before responding and the time per frame gave a further indication of any difficulty. Of course the extra long time for any one frame may be no more than a pupil sharpening his pencil, but if a number of individuals all stop at the same point it is worth looking for the explanation.

There are many time measures that are useful when recorded in this way: the time per frame, the time per lesson, the overall teaching time for the programme, and the variance within and between groups on all these scores. Speed of response has been found to be a sensitive index of the difficulty of particular frames, whilst the overall time is a necessary guide if a teacher is planning a syllabus.

The error-rate may be similarly analysed. The error-rate per individual frame for a group gives us an indication of whether the frame iself is satisfactory in that context; the error-rate per student, whether the programme as a whole is satisfactory for the particular student; and the error-rate per group, whether the programme is suitable for a particular class of students. The overall measure can be misleading, but where it is analysed in some detail to show which particular lessons were difficult and the percentage of students who made mistakes, it is a valuable guide to future revision of the programme and to future users of it.

A further point that has to be considered is the need to examine the errors on a particular frame in relation to preceding material. The difficulty is not always located on the actual error frame but in previous explanatory frames that have been inadequate.

When programmers take all this trouble to analyse responses they naturally must be able to rely on a student's responses being authentic. The whole procedure is useless if in fact the responses are not genuine. For this reason when a text-book format is used for evaluation purposes it has to be appreciated that some cheating may occur. There are several varieties of this behaviour. In a group there will generally be some attempt to help each other, either by blatant copying or whispering of answers. Then there is the looking ahead to see if the response is correct before writing it on paper, or looking ahead to get the answer to try and work it out. Hartley in his research noted some amusing alterations by students where they had originally made correct responses but had changed them when they found a different answer given in the programme, due in this case to a mistake by the printer. It is of course at precisely the difficult points in which the programmer is most interested that such irregularities will occur, and therefore it is advisable to use a cheat-proof presentation, preferably by a machine.

When eventually the author has a programme which his pupils can go through in reasonable time without too many mistakes, how does he decide whether the teaching results are satisfactory? He will of course have his criterion test which will examine how far students have learnt the subject which the programme aimed to teach. This test which may have been given both before and after the programme will show what was already known and what has been learned. Where it can be agreed that the criterion test represents a useful, even worthy acquisition of knowledge, then the value of the teaching programme can be indicated. We can also use the same kind of test to demonstrate whether such knowledge is retained over any length of time.

But the research worker is now much more interested in demonstrating where a programme has taught successfully, where it has failed, and where it could be improved, than in making some overall comparison with the human teacher. It may well be that in its formal role the machine will be cooperating and not competing with the teacher. We have tried to stress that comparative experiments seeking to evaluate teaching methods can only discover their relative efficiency under the conditions of the experiment. Unless one of the methods is incapable of further improvement we would hesitate to predict any permanent advantage to any particular teaching method. What the programmer does well today may become the speciality of the classroom teacher tomorrow. And what the teacher preserves for personal communication may one day seem obviously better done by programmed instruction or methods yet unknown. But whatever the respective future roles of teacher and programmed instruction neither will be successful without the careful research that is gradually building up our knowledge of how to teach, based on a psychology of how we learn. This may seem grandiose when we bring it to earth with the humble task of analysing and reconstructing a programme but the essence of the system is simply that it is self-correcting. We may put this at the elemental level of feedback of individual responses. But the general philosophy of the approach has wider implications for student and teacher and programmer. It is not the making of errors that is important but the recognition that an error has been made. Progress is made, not when an improvement is put forward, but when it is recognized as being superior to the existing method. Efficiency has to be recognized if it is to be a way of life. Programmed instruction accepts this view and tries at every point not to shelter behind the vaguer generalities of educational ideas, but to scrutinize its results and throw out its failures and even its half-successes. It is already making us think about the content as well as the method of our courses. We will return to this in our final chapter.

CHAPTER 8

FUTURE RESEARCH AND DEVELOPMENT

WE have often made the point that these are early days for programmed instruction and the real wonder is that these early models are so effective. They have had some success and now the tendency is to regard them as if they represented fully developed systems in which future changes were unlikely. The research worker holds a very different view. Everywhere in the field of communications he sees new techniques being developed. It is apparently worth investing fortunes to make it possible to speak and see each other over the finite distances of our planet. To do so artificial satellites are put into orbit, radio waves are cunningly bounced back to earth and a whole technology has been developed. In the field of teaching we have lacked this pioneering spirit. We have clung so long to traditional methods, a traditional syllabus and traditional examinations that the modern world has had too little impact upon education. The ripple that has been caused by programmed instruction is really a mark of how stagnant the pool was. In a more vigorous and go-ahead field the contribution of programmed instruction to date should not have been observable.

But now that further teaching methods have been suggested, what of the future? Significant findings are likely to arise directly from research and may well be different from our expectations. We are now able to examine the efforts of manipulating teaching conditions at many points, and we may anticipate that some research workers will be sharp enough to observe the unexpected result and to ask themselves why it has come about. Meanwhile several issues have already arisen: for example, whether a group teaching system could be devised that would be as effective as an individual machine.

GROUP TEACHING SYSTEM

This is controversial, for teaching machines have always stressed the virtues of individual instruction. They were partly devised to meet legitimate criticisms of the classroom, such as students failing to follow a lesson and often having no means of finding out whether they were right or wrong until it was too late to help them. Yet programmes were developed to control students' behaviour and it may be that they are more successful in doing just this than their authors had appreciated. If a programme is made as efficient a teaching instrument as it can be by initial planning and subsequent evaluation, then we may have such a successful technique for controlling student behaviour that we could teach a group together. The matter seemed to us sufficiently open to be worth research.

Accordingly we devised a group system in which the aim was to retain as many as possible of the main features of programmed instruction. It seemed to us that this was possible. For example, material could still be formulated into a logical teaching sequence; the level of the programme could be set for the particular student population to be taught; the programme could be evaluated and rewritten; the interaction between student and material could be maintained; errors could be indicated immediately both to student and teacher and correct responses confirmed; the results could remain private to the individual student and teacher, public failure and success being avoided. The one outstanding feature missing from such a list is that of self-pacing. Individual programmed instruction has always permitted the student to proceed at his own rate but within a group this hardly seemed possible. Perhaps we might return to this point after describing the group machine we constructed.

We use one central display by projecting 35-mm. film. This gives a clear enough image of reading material for all members in the class. Each sits at a student station which is an ordinary desk on which is mounted a small console consisting of four keys and two lights, red and green. Each station is connected to a central control console which registers and holds a student's first response to each frame. When a student responds a 'right' or 'wrong' light comes on at the central console and stays on for the duration of the interval for which the frame is exposed. If the student makes any further responses this is indicated on the lights but does not affect the memory state in the console. At the student station if the correct key is selected the light on his individual console comes on and stays on for that frame. If a wrong key is pressed the wrong light appears, but the student may try again and a correct response will be indicated.

So far, then, the system provides each student with immediate information about his response and allows a correction procedure without destroying information about the first response. Where a linear type of programme is used we have a fixed sequence of frames so the major problem is to determine when to move from one frame to the next. In theory this could be based on a number of criteria. We might move when all students have responded, in which case the slowest member would be setting the pace; or when a fixed percentage of responses are in, which would entail some students not responding. We could have the same fixed time interval for all frames, which would make frame writing extremely difficult, or a set time interval for individual frames. Finally, we might use some combination of the above such as a fixed time interval for frames which is overridden if all responses are made.

There are objections to most of the above, particularly if a group machine is to be used without a teacher being present. It would only require some joker in the class to appreciate that he could hold up the whole class by not responding to bring some of the above procedures to a halt. In order to avoid this we have devised a system that will give students every opportunity to respond but which will advance a frame after a reasonable time has elapsed. It operates as follows. We assume that students' responses in time are normally distributed, that is, are spread out around the average response time in the same bell-shaped curve that is found for stature or intelligence in the population. This allows us to predict on the basis of a few responses how long the remainder should take for any one frame. It is convenient to do this at the fifty per cent point where in a normal distribution the mean, mode and medium points coincide. If we measure the time taken for half the students to respond to a frame we only need to double that amount to predict the total time allowed for that frame. When that time is reached, the frame is advanced, but should every student have responded before the allotted time the frame is automatically moved on. In practice we know that time measures are not normally distributed but it now becomes an empirical matter to examine what proportion of time should be added or subtracted in order that students may have a reasonable opportunity to respond. We have carried out a series of experiments and our preliminary findings indicate that students are being taught satisfactorily and in much the same times as with individual machines.

We recognize that these are paced conditions; a student has a limited if fair time in which to respond. And we make no pretence that this is ideal. But a teacher has to take on considerable responsibility when he decides what he will teach, how he will present it and what he will accept as a satisfactory criterion of learning. Why, then, should he stop short at the rate of presentation of material? The psychologist knows well enough that one of the most effective measures of control is in time and one might argue that it is wasteful to go to such lengths to control behaviour and then permit students to respond as they wish. This after all is not what they will do in 'real life'. People ask questions and expect answers there and then; tasks are given and have to be carried out on the spot. There are certainly good reasons that can be advanced for controlling time, but the basic objection is that a bewildered student may get completely lost and be learning nothing. This is the risk and it is here that a careful system of programming with immediate responses does at least give the student every opportunity to succeed, and where he fails, to indicate immediately that he has done so. One of the impressive features of such a group system is the ease with which even a stranger, watching the central console, can quickly pick out any student who is in difficulties.

The considerable advantage of the system has not yet been mentioned – just money. It is economically a very big saving to build only one projection system for a class of say, thirty, whilst the student stations are relatively cheap units to construct. The

whole system has been devised to produce as economically practical a unit as possible.

CLOCK-PACED SYSTEM

The group teaching system does require at least six to eight
students to be effective but we have developed a clock-paced
system which any number of students, or even a single student
may use. It is suitable for work with either programmed books or
any type of teaching machine. The frames of the programme are
numbered, and in front of the group is a display of up to twenty-
five numbers, which have been selected to cover the range of
frame numbers for that particular programme. These numbers
are illuminated one at a time in numerical order in such a way
as to follow a particular time schedule. Thus the number
twelve might be illuminated after six minutes had elapsed from
the moment the class began the programme. Those who were
past frame number twelve would then know that they were
working rather faster than was intended. Those who had not
reached this frame would know that they ought to be working
faster. In our experiments we recorded how the most successful
students allotted their time as they went through the programme.
With the short linear frames we were using, a good student would
average at least two frames per minute, spending somewhat
longer on the difficult items and speeding up wherever the programme became easier or the frames shorter. So we arranged for
our clock to display to groups of students the timetable or time
schedule created by combining the records of students who had
learned successfully from the programme. We based the schedule
on the best and fastest students because we wanted to see what
effect the clock would have if it moved on rather quicker than
many of our students would have selected for themselves.

The result was that all our students finished the programme
before the clock had finished its sequence of displays. This meant
that all our trial students were working at least as fast as the best
of the students who had used the same programme at their own
pace. And their final test scores were identical. Our detailed records showed that some students prefer to keep very close to the

clock schedule, others like to race on and get as far ahead as possible. By deliberately speeding up the clock and later slowing it down, we were able to show that our students were taking notice of the clock and were making serious efforts to catch up if they discovered that they were behind schedule. We were surprised that when interviewed after the experiment, every student expressed a preference for the clock-paced system over the free-paced use of programmed books which was their normal method of programmed learning. They all said that the clock showed them at any moment where they stood and this reassured them that they were working at the right pace.

There are two main disadvantages with the clock-paced teaching system, one of them purely technical. It requires a 'programmed' clock which can present a different schedule for each programme, and perhaps for different classes using the same programme, and the programmer has to decide on the schedule in advance with the attendant risk of encouraging the students to work faster or slower than they should. The group teaching system, as we have seen, does not have to be provided with a time schedule in advance because it uses a voting procedure to decide when to move on. To use the clock-paced system efficiently, the programmer must find out the optimum time schedule for each programme, for each type of programmed book or teaching machine he intends to use, and for each type of class if there are pronounced differences. Thus for pacing purposes, each programme should have a series of *evaluated* times which are the recommended times in which students of the target population should complete the various sections of the programme.

In some cases it is certainly true that a student can be working too fast or too slow for his own good. And he may not realize this unless he knows the optimum or evaluated rate for that programme. Going too slowly can be a severe strain on remembering where it unduly lengthens the learning time – if a student works at a snail's pace he may have completely forgotten the beginning by the time he reaches the end. On the other hand, the speedy worker is sometimes, but not always, the careless one who makes mistakes and may learn falsely or not at all simply because he was going too fast to notice a crucial point.

From a research point of view, we see the clock-paced system as a way of urging students to work faster in order to find out how fast they have to work before their results start to suffer. Once we have discovered the optimum rate of working or the optimum time schedule for a particular programme, it may not be necessary to do more than tell the student at various points in the programme how much time he should have spent on the previous section and how much he should spend on the next. This will give him a very clear idea of how hard to work and serve as a guide to the importance of the materials he is studying.

So far we have discussed developments in programming itself which we might sum up as efforts to give us the maximum flexibility, compatible with costs, to meet the individual needs of a student. We are, and shall be, teaching huge numbers of students so that group techniques have to be explored. It may well be that such methods will be used in conjunction with radio or television to reach wider audiences. And this is particularly challenging for we are trying to unite two systems that on the surface seem incompatible. Radio and television are typical examples of twentieth-century communication systems of the open loop type, with no built-in facility for feedback from receiver to sender, whilst teaching machines are an extreme example of the opposite approach, a closed loop system. But if we do use carefully evaluated programmed material we may well achieve a much higher degree of control over students' learning than is usual in such broadcasting exercises, and this could then be taken a step further on the lines of the integrated programming method we discussed in Chapter 6. There is a great temptation for television instruction to concentrate upon the eye-catching, spectacular demonstration and leave understanding in the background. Programmed material, that had been carefully evaluated, would be a safeguard on this score, and where it could be followed up by classroom instruction so that we had a fully integrated system there is no doubt that we should have a powerful teaching method. Close co-operation between the programmed instruction writer, the broadcasting and teaching staff could go far to ensure its success. And even where there was no teaching staff to follow up the broadcast, the student receiving the programmed instruction would still be in a much better position to assess his own progress than he is at present.

There is no doubt that further efforts will be made along these lines as the sheer quantity of information and skill to be taught increases. There seems every chance that our teaching system will reach the limits of its capacity, and we cannot always raise the school-leaving age. Faced with an emergency two possibilities seem open to us, one of which is the development of improved methods of teaching, of which we like to think programmed instruction is a good example. The other is a revision of what has to be taught either by simply deleting topics – always a bone of contention – or by rearranging the conceptual structure of a subject matter in order to speed up the teaching. A good example of the latter is the current trend to reorganize mathematics teaching by bringing set theory down from the postgraduate level and using it in a fundamental way at the primary level. By thus taking a different approach to the basic concepts of a topic the quantity which can be mastered in a given time has been increased.

We may illustrate the significance of assessing what exactly are the aims of a syllabus by considering a homely example of how to teach cookery. The normal method is to learn a relatively small number of recipes on which only minor variations are practised throughout the career of the 'cook'. A slightly more advanced method advocated by some cookery authors is for the cook to master certain basic skills and recipes such as producing plainly cooked food, roasted, boiled, grilled, steamed, fried, and cold. Add a set of multi-purpose sauces and dressings and your trainee cook would have a creditable repertoire. The third approach would be to study all recipes and methods of preparing food in order to identify the 'principles' and basic facts. One would find a fairly small set of principles and a large set of facts which could be arranged in various ways. For example, the preparation, food value, the flavour, the cost and availability of each possible ingredient would constitute a set of basic facts with which the perfect cook ought to be familiar.

Now if we could manage to teach or make easily available all these facts and if the trainee could be given mastery of the principles of food preparation, then we would have a cook of a very different kind to the one who merely knows a handful of recipes and the location of the nearest frozen food supplier. Our true cook would be able to invent dishes to suit the available ingredients and the target population. A shortage of one item would be overcome by the use of another.

What we are illustrating by our example is the benefit of a careful study of what should be taught. The analysis of a curriculum will almost certainly be a difficult and costly process; but its benefits should be considerable. A good curriculum will assist all pupils. A redundant item will waste the time and efforts of all who struggle to master it. We wish to imply that a well-designed curriculum identifies the important intellectual skills and often relegates the factual content to a different level, that is the learner knows how to locate but does not necessarily try to remember the actual material. Facts easily available in a convenient reference source need not be committed to memory. Is an examination a test of skill or of rote memory? A craftsman learns to use his tools and can thereafter tackle any job. The component assembler learns to work very quickly but may have to begin learning again when the component is changed.

There is clearly a balance to be struck between learning specific facts or operations and developing more generally applicable skills. As an educational system reaches its limiting capacity, so a small shift in this point of balance can make a large difference in the abilities of the graduating students. Thus it has come about that people interested in self-correcting teaching systems have come to the conclusion that once a system is working reasonably well, a change in the curriculum will often be more useful to the students than an improvement in the teaching methods. This can be reduced to the truism that the best teaching machine is useless if it contains the wrong programme.

We therefore wish to stress that there are important matters of curriculum design which have been under consideration for many years. The teaching machine has probably given this work some unexpected but justified publicity. We feel that it is necessary to be on guard lest teaching becomes an end in itself and the curriculum design studies are important reminders. We will mention one of them as being representative. It is a military study which is important as a model of how industrial training could be organized.

The study was conducted by the Human Resources Research Office at the George Washington University. This research office has conducted many specific projects on Army training and the staff decided that the time had come to look at their work as a whole and attempt to predict its future directions. They refer to this kind of activity as Generalized Training Research, and this is primarily an identification of the issues on which future research would be likely to be most useful

The preliminary analysis stage was designed to categorize the training, personnel selection, and other requirements of a selected group of Army jobs. Combat jobs were the group chosen because of their obvious priority. The final analysis stage distinguished within the jobs themselves the particular knowledge and skills required, but it also determined across a range of jobs how general or how specific were these attributes.

By a careful and detailed examination of what was entailed in each job the researchers were able to list in order of importance the 'topics' which were required in the selected group of combat jobs. The significance of this type of analysis was that the training research units were not only able to identify the key knowledges and skills required in combat jobs, but thereby could concentrate on improving training in these areas, knowing that any finding would be extensively applied.

Suppose we speculate about a parallel study in industry and commerce. What is the topic of greatest generality throughout all the jobs? What are the top twenty knowledges and skills? Given only an approximate ranking we would be in a position to deploy our limited resources so as to make best use of them. And from this list of the most generally used knowledges and skills we would be able to evaluate both our training and educational system in so far as it has to prepare its pupils both for an immediate vocation and probably other employments during their working careers. It seems highly unlikely that the majority of our workers will continue in the jobs of their first choice throughout their working careers, for it is clear that such jobs will inevitably undergo changes during the next two or three decades.

CHAPTER 9

COMPUTER-ASSISTED INSTRUCTION

WE will begin by an example of computer instruction. The following is a short conversation between computer and student during the course of a simple logic game.

The computer 'thinks' of a letter of the alphabet. The player's task is to discover which letter this is. He is allowed to ask questions. For example, he might ask 'How many curves?' or 'How many loose ends?' The letter X, for example, has no curves and four loose ends whereas the letter P has one curve and only one loose end. The player could also ask about other characteristics of the letter such as horizontals, verticals or obliques. If the letter was X he would receive the reply that it had no horizontals, no verticals and two obliques. Only one question can be asked at a time and the object of the game is to identify the letter positively with as few questions as possible.

Here is the conversation.

COMPUTER: Start when ready.
STUDENT: Curves?
C. One
S. Loose ends?
C. Two
S. Obliques?
C. Zero
S. C [*Meaning* C *is the answer*]
C. You don't have enough information yet to get the right answer. How do you know it isn't J for example?
Note: The computer will not accept a guess from the student if he did not have enough information to specify the correct answer.
This is a logic game not a guessing game.
S. J

c. You don't have enough information yet. How do you know it isn't C for example?

s. Horizontals?

c. Zero. That was a wasted question. It did not eliminate any possibilities.

s. Verticals?

c. Zero. Good question.

s. G

c. Wrong. Your guess is inconsistent with the information you've been given. You must have forgotten that the right letter hasn't any horizontal lines. The letter you guessed can't be right – it has two many loose ends.

s. Curves?

c. The answer is still: one.

s. X

c. Wrong. Your guess is inconsistent with the information you've been given. I think you only made that guess to see what I would say.

s. C

c. Yes, you've done it. Good work. If you want to play again, start right in.*

This example illustrates how the interaction between teaching system and student becomes more meaningful when the system can take previous transactions into account and relate them to the present response or inquiry. More simple teaching machines can, of course, relate the teaching to the material which has already been exposed to the student, but they can relate it in only a limited way to his previous responses. The example indicates how the logical capabilities of a computer can be used to detect such things as redundancy in questions and inconsistency in conclusions which can be immediately brought to the student's attention. We hope it will serve as an example of the kind of teaching that is possible with computers and be a reminder that this type of teaching can be both exciting and informative.

In this chapter we propose to discuss some features of computers that are important for teaching, and the kind of hardware

* This example, and the following on p. 145 is based on the examples given by Swets and Feurweig in *Science*, vol. 150, 29 October 1965.

that would be necessary for a teaching system. We are all aware that remarkable advances are taking place in computer technology and it is only too easy to be dazzled by these possibilities and to lose sight of the goal. But there is little doubt that computers are here to stay and to have wider applications by taking on what have hitherto been human functions. If we pause, then, to look at the general trends of their development and consider the general characteristics of computers we may be able to answer the query whether they are likely to take on the very human function of teaching.

Over the last decade computers have become more powerful and at the same time physically much smaller and cheaper. There is, as yet, no generally accepted formula for measuring the power of a computer, but it is related to its cycle speed, the efficiency of its compiling programme and the size of its fast access or 'core' store. Ten years ago computers were fast; given a thousandth part of a second they could carry out some five additions. Today a fast machine can cope with about 500 such operations in this time. And the limit has not yet been reached. Whereas we now measure cycle speeds in millionths of a second it is already certain that with future machines we will need to measure in fractions of a millionth. This remarkable increase in speed has been brought about by the change from the thermionic valve to solid state switching techniques.

The second factor affecting the power of a computer is the efficiency of its compiling programme. Computers carry out the instructions they are given in what is called machine code. The programmer could write his programmes in this machine code, but they would be very long and complicated. To overcome this problem, various programming languages have been developed to allow the programmer to write in a language closer to English than machine code. To use one of these programming languages the computer first reads in a compiling programme which thereafter translates the programme written in the special language into machine code. The reader might well ask why compiling programmes have not been written which will allow the programmer to write in plain English. But spoken or written English is far from being plain, if by plain we mean simple in its logical structure.

The meaning of a word or phrase depends so much on the context in which it occurs, whilst ambiguity has often been deliberate. Even simple words have several meanings. When confronted with pens do we write with them or keep sheep in them? A compiler programme would have to make such material intelligible to a system as 'literal-minded' as a computer. Even were it possible to construct such a compiler its size would be enormous.

As the programming language gets closer to English so the size of the compiler programme increases. Now the computer has to keep all the compiler in its store so the situation could arise where a computer was so full of compiler that it had no room left for working space. Therefore programmers must settle for languages more limited and more formally structured than everyday English where each statement which is allowed has a precise literal meaning. Even then such languages demand quite large compilers and programmers are always on the look-out for ways of improving their efficiency by reducing their size and compiling speed, without sacrificing their ability to accept a particular programming language.

The other important factor contributing to power, the size of the fast access information store, has shown a corresponding advance. Core stores which can hold many millions of bits of information are now considered practical.

But this tremendous increase in power has been accompanied, not by an increase but by a startling decrease in physical size. A machine built a few years ago which fills a large room can now be replaced by one of equivalent or greater power which will be no larger than a desk. In another few years such a machine will sit comfortably on a table top.

But what of price? Here again there has been a dramatic decrease. Often price is measured in £s per bit (binary unit). Eight to ten years ago £2 per bit was the order of things; today it is well under £1 and with the larger systems possibly as low as 2/6d. per bit. If we consider an actual case, a university purchased a computer eight years ago at a cost of £100,000. It is now being replaced by a more powerful (and also physically smaller) machine. This computer will cost four times as much but it can do sixty times as much work. Price per unit power has come down by a factor of fifteen. This is one of the few areas where money is buying more as time goes by.

If we now turn to the functions of a computer we may appreciate why we are often confused about this kind of machine. A machine is defined by its functions, and since many machines can only do one thing this is straightforward enough. A table fork is a machine for carrying food to the mouth. But we are used to the idea of machines having more than one function. We expect a hand-drilling machine to be used as a drill, but we accept the idea that if the cutting tool is replaced by a polishing mop the same rotary action will function as a polisher. We have changed the function of the machine by changing a part of the machine. Now the computer is slightly different. What the computer does is determined by its programme, that is, by a set of instructions which can be fed into it, and which it will carry out. If we change from one computer programme, say, for doing stock control, to another for doing language translation we have altered the function and in a real sense we have a different machine. But unlike the case of our drill and polisher we have not changed the parts to change its function. This is exactly the case with the general purpose computer. It is not so much one machine as a potential for building a number of different machines by employing different computer programmes. We build a new machine, that is we construct a device for carrying out a specified set of functions, not by using a soldering iron but by knowing how to instruct the computer to perform the precise functions we wish.

The computer itself has, of course, a set of fixed or basic functions and it is these that are called into play by instructions from the programme. Each of these functions is in itself a simple enough move, and in digital computers is based upon a system of binary choices, yes or no answers, that are symbolized by a 1 or 0 notation. By means of the binary system a computer may carry out the standard and very fast arithmetic operations that we associate with it, but it is more important that it provides a logical language which permits the computer to answer a variety of questions. It is in this sense that a computer is a general purpose machine for processing data or information, and is able to perform surprisingly complex functions involving interrelated decisions.

These are desirable and even necessary features if the computer is to be part of a teaching system, especially if one imagines a teaching system which follows closely the progress of each student and tries to lead him through the subject by supplying just the right information or encouragement at each moment in the learning process. Such a system may seem quite fantastic compared with the 'essay tonight and mark it next week' type of teaching, but this is precisely the kind of operation that computers are controlling in other fields. For example, their industrial uses are quite spectacular. Computers control the characteristics of steel strip coming out of a rolling mill, or control the drilling of intricate patterns in steel plate, but the computer can only do this when peripheral equipment has been added which acts, so to speak, as its physical limbs and sensing devices. When a computer is controlling a chemical processing plant it is necessary to ensure such factors as rate of flow, temperature and pressure, and to translate these measurements into signals which can be 'understood' by a computer. These signals are fed into the computer through its interface equipment. Similarly, if the computer is to respond to these signals and act back on the process more devices are necessary to convert the instruction signals from the computer into action at the plant itself. To couple the computer to its environment is a fairly complex process requiring obvious technical skill, but once the coupling has been achieved the control is determined by the particular computer programme that is being used, and these control rules may be altered by changes to the programme.

We have already commented on the extraordinary speed of normal computer operations but where the computer is being used on-line with other equipment such as controlling a processing plant, the computer is working in 'real-time'. That is to say, however fast a computer may be performing its own operations it cannot speed on to the next stage but has to wait for the normal cycle time of the operation itself and then take the actual data as the process itself produces them. Now since the speed of the operation will generally be slow indeed, compared with the computer's operating time, the computer will be standing idle for most of its working day. This, however, is overcome by time sharing, when the computer takes on further jobs such as working out the company's wage sheets during intervals when it is not occupied with the process. The odd couple of seconds is a long time to a computer and it can switch easily enough from one programme to another providing the priorities are given to it.

A computer can clearly be used on-line in this way to control teaching and since each student will only be making responses intermittently – say about two every minute – it is easy enough for the computer to handle the responses from a class of students, say twenty or thirty. The increasing numbers do not change the nature of the problem but only make it a more economical process. Basically what is happening is that the computer is asked to store large quantities of information and must call upon this whenever it is required to make a decision. This is precisely what a computer is designed to do, both accurately and speedily. It can detect where a student is making a mistake and whether it is related to any previous misunderstanding, and it can respond appropriately to these errors. It will permit an extremely flexible type of programme. With the ordinary type of programmed teaching system we can insert key frames so that where a student cannot respond he is directed to revise a previous section of material. But the computer may keep a running score of a student's progress and select the next frame on the basis of this total information.

The flexibility of the computer system is neatly illustrated when it is using an interrogation type of programme. For example, suppose a medical student is being taught how to diagnose the illness of a patient. The computer may give the student a list of symptoms and then ask what further information the student would like. He may ask for something that is irrelevant and be told so; he may ask for something that he could have deduced from the data already given and again this can be explained to him; or he may not have a clue what to do next in which case he says so and is given a hint. So the diagnosis can proceed and the computer verifies that the student is not only asking for the relevant information but also that he appreciates the significance of it when it is given. Again the computer can keep a check on the actual time the student is taking and ensure the patient does not 'die' while the student is making up his mind. It can be made into a realistic problem for the student.

The following is an extract from a dialogue between student and computer in such a case. Our extract starts at the point where the student has already asked a number of preliminary questions and from the nature of them has been identified by the computer as a capable student.

COMPUTER: Before proceeding with the re-examination it might be instructive to pause and consider the diagnostic implications of the information at hand. Perhaps you think it too early to arrive at any definitive conclusion. On the other hand, you may be prepared to make the diagnosis now. Are you?

STUDENT: NO.

C. Fine. Nevertheless, we've got a fair amount of information – at least enough to raise some, perhaps several, diagnostic possibilities. Have you any in mind?

S. YES.

C. Name one.

S. PNEUMOCOCCAL PNEUMONIA.

C. Good. The general signs of a pneumonic process are present. Of course, you haven't isolated the bug. Do you think the belly pain and flank pain reinforce the case for pneumococcal pneumonia?

S. NO.

C. Right. Though the white count is consistent, isn't it?

S. YES.

C. I think so too, but a later reading is indicated to confirm this finding. We've considered one possibility. Do you have another diagnosis in mind?

S. NO.

C. In that case I'd like to talk about pulmonary infarction. What I like about that diagnosis is the presence of high fever, rusty sputum, and shaking chills; I don't like the dyspnea, pleural pain, and signs of consolidation – do you agree?

S. NO.

c. You're quite correct. I was just trying to see whether or not you were alert – and you were. Now let's see how the patient is today. Begin the physical when you're ready.

[*Deleted: requests for general appearance and vital signs.*]

s. PNEUMOCOCCAL PNEUMONIA.

c. Yes. I remember you liked this diagnosis before. Are you absolutely sure?

s. NO.

c. What would help you nail down the diagnosis?

s. EVIDENCE FROM SPUTUM SMEAR AND CULTURE.

c. Good. Anything else?

s. EVIDENCE FROM X-RAY FINDINGS.

c. Good. X-ray shows area of consolidation at right lower lobe, consistent with a pneumonic process. Lab reports Grampositive organisms in the sputum smear and the presence of pneumococci in the culture. Had you thought to rule out things like appendicitis and acute pyelonephritis? Apparently you weren't thrown off by the referred abdominal pain. In any case, you've made the correct diagnosis.

It will be appreciated that this form of interrogation is applicable to many subject matters and indeed one of the more spectacular examples we came across was where recruits were being taught to be police detectives and were trying to find the relevant clues in a murder hunt. It is not surprising that these basic procedures are applicable to so much material for we are following a student's deductive thinking and giving him the opportunity to find the answer for himself, even if it takes him a long time. This is a clear cut example of where a computer-controlled method is not only teaching but is seen to be teaching by all the best methods. Socrates himself never played it so fairly as the computer does in its interrogation game – but then Socrates, as a teacher, cheated his students outrageously.

It may be useful at this point to describe a specific example of a computer-based system, always remembering that other systems have used different kinds of hardware and types of programme. One automatic teaching system which has been developed over several years at the Co-ordinated Science Laboratory at the

University of Illinois is PLATO (Programmed Logic for Automatic Teaching Operations). It uses a high-speed digital computer as the central control element for teaching a number of students simultaneously, while still allowing each student to proceed independently through the material.

The rules governing the teaching process are included in the programme written for the central computer and are known as the teaching logic. At Illinois two types of teaching logic have been examined, a 'tutorial' logic and an 'inquiry' logic. In the tutorial logic a student follows a fixed sequence of topics, but there are branching facilities that the student controls. The material is first presented to a student, and then questions are asked about it. The student composes his answers and, when ready, asks the computer for a judgement. The student may himself decide to branch to easier material if he is experiencing difficulty, or he may be branched by the computer programme if he fails to meet predetermined criteria.

The 'inquiry' teaching logic is more in the nature of a dialogue between student and computer. Typically general problems are presented to the student who has to solve them by requesting appropriate information from the computer. Of course where the student knows the material he has only to answer the questions and move on to the next matter.

In order to handle these systems the following equipment has been developed. Each student communicates with the central computer by an electronic keyset. This is like a typewriter keyboard, where the alphanumeric characters are assigned positions similar to those on a standard typewriter, whilst the extra characters are given the particular control functions the designer wishes. Thus each student can transmit words, numerals, sentences or algebraic expressions. In turn each student receives information from the computer on a television screen. This information may be derived from two sources. In one, known as the 'electronic book', slides stored in a random access slide selector are controlled by the computer; the other is a more complicated means known as an 'electronic blackboard'. Here diagrams, symbols and words are plotted in a point-by-point fashion and this allows them to be kept in the information stores instead of on films or Videotape.

A block diagram of the system is shown in Figure 13. This illustrates the flow of information from the computer to the student and in turn from the student to the computer. The system, as we have discussed it, only allows for one student operating with a computer but in practice this would be quite uneconomical and PLATO has been designed so that students can work simultaneously upon different subject matter. Figure 13 illustrates this for two students but many more could be accommodated. Indeed it is claimed 'that a general purpose computer, having a high-speed capacity of 1·5 million bits, would allow 1,000 students to be tutored concurrently on eight different lessons without incurring a noticeable delay on any student's request'. Of course a computer of 1·5 million bits capacity is large but it will be clear that where we employ large-scale equipment it need not be for one or two students.

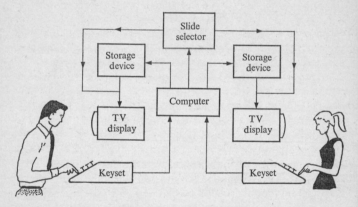

Figure 13. Block diagram for computer teaching system (PLATO)

But the converse question is economically more interesting; how far can we reduce computer size and still teach the number of students we wish? It is certainly the case in Britain, and in many European countries if not in the United States, that we are often wanting to teach relatively small classes of students – say hirty to fifty. The key problem with the smaller computer in at teaching role is how do we store sufficient data. Any serious subject matter will take up so much programme that it would be quite impossible to take up computer space to store it. And even the alternative of using peripheral digital data stores such as disc files is feasible for only limited material, and not very practical for visual material.

In such situations it is fairly clear that conventional information stores must be used: libraries, films, tape-recorders. What the computer will have to do is to direct the student to search out for himself the relevant item, study it, and return for a diagnostic question session with the computer. We will return to this problem when we consider how different data are stored.

THE COMPUTER IN A TEACHING, EDITING AND STATISTICAL MODE

We have spoken of computers as both providing the teaching material for a student and keeping a record of his learning performance. A computer will in fact perform a variety of functions that we should distinguish, for together they will enable us to control a student's course of instruction in such a way that not only will he himself derive maximum benefit but also the instructional process itself will profit by experience. Future generations must also be taught!

In practice this depends upon the kinds of information we can derive from the teaching system. A computer system will try to meet the individual's special needs which means that it must be well informed about each individual that it teaches. It must be able to detect and remedy his special difficulties, decide whether he is doing himself justice or under-achieving in relation to his abilities. But it must also be collating information about the general effectiveness of the course, how quickly it is teaching all its students, where they experience difficulty, whether they are able to cope with test problems. This implies that the system must not only meet the needs of the individual student by storing, retrieving and acting upon information in accordance with its programmed set of instructions, it must also be able to operate in various modes. We may call these a teaching mode, a programme editing mode, and a statistical mode.

In the *teaching mode* the computer system is closest in its operation to other programmed methods. It issues teaching materials in the form of frames or work assignments to a student, it marks tests and makes comments on his progress along the lines we have indicated, and it is particularly suited to use an interrogation type of method.

In the *editing mode* the system is available to the tutor or instructor so that he can bring up to date any part of the teaching programme as appears necessary. He can modify the operating instructions, change the criteria, or even rewrite sections of the actual teaching programme that are not proving satisfactory. Such information is mainly provided by the computer in its *statistical mode*. The system can give information about the work standards of any or all of its students, it may provide data on the efficiency of the various teaching sections, or the reliability of tests. It is in these two latter modes that the computer offers unique facilities. As a teaching unit it is more flexible than other programming systems, but as a continuous provider of information about the on-going course of teaching it is unique among existing systems. For example, in a large school how many teachers could honestly say how much a particular student knew about one specific course, which questions he could and could not answer? A computer could provide the information rapidly for any or all of its students and on the basis of its collated experience suggest the remedial measures that were necessary.

In order to function in these different modes a computer must store and handle a great variety of data. We will distinguish two kinds, content data and control data.

Content data refer to the subject matter being taught. 'Cats are carnivores' might be a piece of content data in a system teaching zoology. Tests requiring a student to respond – for example, 'Are cats carnivores?' – will also be classified as content data although their function is to elicit information from a student. Also under the heading of content data will come comments which might be issued to a student – 'Your score on that test was above average', or 'Try to speed up your working.'

It will be apparent that we have listed under content data all information which is to be communicated to a student, whether it is written, spoken, or in diagrams. But this type of data need not be in a form which has been directly stored within the computer system; all that is required is that it can be issued on instruction. Such data may have been stored in a variety of ways – slides, continuous film, tape-recorder – but they are called upon by the computer as required.

Control data refer to information which will be used to control the teaching. The computer instructions which determine which content data should be issued at any one time will call upon control data to make this decision. For example, a computer instruction might, if translated into an English sentence, read, 'If the present student spent less than the average time taken by previous students on the last 50 frames and scored less than 75 per cent on the current test, issue comment No. 20, if he spent more than this time issue comment No. 25, otherwise continue with teaching frame No. 172.'

To act on this instruction the computer would need to have stored previous students' times on the prescribed frames and calculated the average time. These data, together with data referring to the present student's time and his test score, would need to be in a form which the computer itself could interpret. It will be clear from the above example that the system need not interpret the content of the teaching frames, test and comments, but is only required to call them up by code numbers. Control data will therefore include such things as test scores, time on frames and tests, and possibly information about a student's previous study courses, measured aptitudes and so on.

SOME TECHNICAL CONSIDERATIONS

There are obviously different constraints on the form of storage required for the two types of data we have just mentioned. These, together with economic considerations determine the actual storage techniques adopted in any system. Without in any way providing a detailed technical guide to computer operations we will indicate briefly how these functions are usually carried out.

DATA STORAGE

The heart of the computer is the core store. The instructions which the computer obeys and the data on which it is immediately operating must be available here. As we noted, storage is in binary form, so we can view the core as a large set of on–off switches. It is in fact magnetic in operation and consequently very fast with no moving parts.

Core store is, however, expensive so that we have to add further peripheral equipment to increase storage capacity. This involves such items as disc-files and magnetic drums. Here the price per bit of peripheral storage is much less than with core store, but access to the data is slower and might take thousandths rather than millionths of a second. Clearly when using a system to teach students this slight loss of speed need be no problem unless we are sharing computer time between very many students.

Control data which have to be interpreted by the computer must be available in binary form in the core store if they are to be utilized for decision making. Almost any size of system would need to store a large quantity of control data (e.g. computer instructions for running a number of teaching programmes, data about each of many students, and recorded data about the performance of students for future appraisal and evaluation of the teaching materials and decisions). Therefore the most practical form of storage would probably be the disc-file.

On the other hand, content data must be presented to a student in a convenient and meaningful form, but need not be meaningful within the control system. Here we have a real choice of storage systems. The data may be stored on disc-file and translated by the computer into written English, or whatever the teaching language might be. Alternatively, the content may be stored in some form such as film (as with some teaching machines) or tape-recorders. The only restriction is that the computer can issue an instruction which will result in the appropriate message being produced for the student. For example, the instruction to a film store might be 'Go to frame 189' or to a tape-recorder 'Go to message 75.' What then appears before the student may be Greek or grammar, depending upon the particular frame in the particular programme that is selected.

There are pros and cons to both methods. If we choose to store content data in binary form on a disc-file we must involve the computer in the task of translating this into written language for the student. Although the computer can do this very quickly we could run into queueing problems when the system is large, that is, where it has to handle many students at one time. Computers are very fast in their operating speeds but the printed output to a student is slow by comparison. Teleprinters usually type at about one hundred words per minute. This is quite fast enough to keep a student happy but, in view of the mismatch in speed between the printer and computer, it is necessary to insert devices called 'buffers' to hold the necessary information and let the computer get on with its other work whilst the teleprinter is writing its message. Another limitation is the difficulty of presenting diagrams or photographs when using teleprinter output. Data which are stored in digital form can be displayed on an oscilloscope screen (rather like a TV screen). This requires further equipment but it allows sentences, numbers or graphs to be displayed. For many purposes however such graphic materials can be stored on slides or film and projected to the student on command from the computer.

As a large number of students will have to be taught concurrently by any realistic system the problem of addressing each of them individually at their own station must be solved. The computer has to switch rapidly from one student source to another and this is achieved by devices known as multiplexers. For a large number of students buffer and multiplexer systems will have to be developed. It is not necessary to be an expert in the technical field to appreciate that such devices will be both complex and expensive. These problems have been met but their solution does require considerable expensive hardware and we should not close our eyes to it.

THE COMPUTER AS A TEACHER

But if we now turn from technicalities of computers we may fairly ask what special features and advantages does the computer-controlled system offer for teaching. In many respects the computer method is similar to ordinary programmed instruction. A student will receive a carefully prepared course, he will be required to work actively at it and be informed about his progress from time to time. And in one sense a computer-assisted teaching system can offer nothing further. Yet if we look more closely at the details there are differences in degree which to the student and to the teacher will appear as qualitative differences.

Consider first the moment-to-moment activity of the system. Marking tests, however tedious for a human teacher, is micro-work for the computer. Therefore the student can have the luxury of detailed and up-to-date knowledge of how he is progressing. Tabulating results over many students is easy for the computer so the learner can be told how he is progressing compared with his peers. And all this can happen several times per lesson rather than only after terminal examinations when it is too late to take remedial action. Where a system can have a large library of lessons, remedial action can be taken by offering the student who is in difficulties just the material he needs to overcome them. This is a big improvement over a conventional branching programme with its handful of remedial frames for those who choose particular wrong answers. This raises another point with which the computer can deal. Branching normally takes place on the basis of whether a single response is right or wrong. Anything more complicated would tax the teaching machine and prohibit the reliable use of scrambled books. Yet a simple decision process in the computer could allow the teacher to plan for such contingencies as the student who is working well but too slowly, or the fast, careless worker who needs to slow down, or the pupil whose records suggest that he should be given more challenging material.

We thus see a picture of a sensitive teaching system which to the student behaves as a superbly well-informed tutor, offering information and tailor-made guidance based on the equivalent of long personal experience. This is the paradox of a computer-assisted system. It responds to the particular performance of a student and therefore has the features of close personal supervision. This level of sophistication may appear to be outside present-day capabilities, but the details are quite ordinary matters which, one by one, a competent teacher would take in his stride. Yet to expect him to deal with all these details all the time for all his students is clearly too much for one man alone.

Consider now the system, not from the point of view of the student, but the teacher. We have emphasized the fact that computer-assisted instruction in its statistical role offers the teacher a fast, competent clerical assistant. Here the computer is changing its role from class minder to technical assistant. How this assistant uses the actual teaching materials, and of course the materials themselves, are under the direction of the teacher. The teacher will have the responsibility of quizzing the computer.

Suppose a teacher has just set up a new computer-assisted course. The first thing he will ask the computer is for a print-out of the final test results to see how the course is going. He will then ask for individual students' records and timetables. If he suspects a certain part of his course, he may ask for tabulated error responses for this section. Thus he can get a detailed picture of how his course is teaching. Naturally he will improve it where he can. And it is a relatively trivial matter to ask the computer to keep a closer watch on certain students, or sections of programme, in order to learn more about the difficult parts of the course.

So we see the computerized system from the teacher's point of view as a device for capturing what is good in the course, and speedily updating what is not. Ordinary programmes do this to some extent but the computer programme may be designed specifically to allow the teacher to experiment in this way. And future generations of students will get the benefit of the improvements.

Now let us take the next step. Let us assume that teaching is an experimental procedure. The teacher composes frames, phrases, diagrams, demonstrations, and offers them to the student in the hope that they will facilitate his learning. If they fail then something else must be tried; if they succeed then on to the next part of the syllabus. But how about letting the computer do the experimenting? If we put in the basic materials, lay down the fundamental rules of procedure, why should we not instruct the computer to experiment and build up courses to suit each student.

This brings us up sharply against our limitations. They are not in the computer but in our knowledge of teaching. The problem is finding out what should comprise the basic materials. Whole lessons are too big as building blocks for teaching, and single words or diagrams are usually too small. The difficulty may be appreciated if we examine a particular example. In the case of the adaptive teaching machine in our own laboratory, Sime has built a device to teach the specific skill of operating a binary-coded keyboard. Subjects had five keys and had to learn which combination of keys to press in order to punch out on tape any particular letter. Now in such a case the total subject matter is limited to the letters of the alphabet and there is no hierarchical structure in the material that demands any one letter combination to be taught before any other. All letters may therefore be put in the programme independently, and we have only to state the decision rules that will determine the selection of an item to begin teaching. In this case the decision rules are simple enough – to present letters for coding in a random order, but to repeat after a stated number of intervening items any letter to which the response was slow. The number of intervening items – 2, 3, 4 and 5 – was determined after trials and the response to any letter was designated as 'slow' if its time was longer than the mean for the whole series.

Under these conditions the machine taught magnificently and certainly reduced the variance in performance between subjects. But the most interesting point was that the machine produced a different programme for each student, based on his individual learning research. The only possible way to improve such a schedule would be by improving the decision rules upon which the machine's choices are based. Now it is precisely our lack of knowledge of the best decision rules in complicated teaching situations that is holding us back. Once we know we should be able to incorporate them into existing systems.

Of course everyday teaching situations are often more complicated than the one we have just outlined. Nevertheless even now it will be possible to cope with subject matter where the units are independent, and in some instances where they are serially ordered, as in mathematics. It will be necessary in these latter instances to 'package' the material in larger units so that the machine may select items that are related. We are only at the beginning of such problems, but at least the machine has made it clear how little we know about how we want our material organized. Once we know what to tell it to do the logic of the system will do the rest.

Up to this point we have been talking about the computer as a device for assembling lessons which either in one form are already partly sequenced by an expert teacher, whilst in the other the computer assembles the sequences of basic units upon the results of testing the student's progress. As a final example which may give some indication of the fascinating possibilities in this field let us consider how the student may be developing his own lesson materials. When speaking of young children we call this play. Adults, too, are sometimes allowed to play with ideas and materials, but they usually refer to this activity by some other name – thinking, projections, research and so on. We are really considering how a computer may be set up as a general-purpose toy, and behind the suggestion are ideas derived from watching how we learn from everyday activities. For example, a child will teach itself set theory with rubbish and a cardboard box, or develop an appreciation for melody by playing with a series of tune fragments and nonsense noises. A set of boffins when they get some new apparatus, such as a computer, demonstrate quickly enough that playing is a potent form of learning. If we can take this situation into education there are countless opportunities for learning by self-controlled play which a computer assisted system would be able to offer. For example, in mathematics we might ask the computer something like 'Plot me the graph of $y = x^3 + 4x^2 - 10x$.' This graph then appears on the output channel, which is here something like a television screen. If now we ask for the values to be changed the curve on the screen would change oo. We may suggest to a student that he tries out a series of values for himself so that he may build up his understanding and appreciation of what it is he is manipulating. With the very high speeds available, it becomes feasible to ask for all sorts of routine calculations and manipulations.

The final results are achieved by large numbers of decisions and actions which in themselves are quite ordinary. But when combined in huge quantities at high speed the effect is unrecognizably different from the elementary, almost crude components. And this is very typical of computer work; so often they are merely achieving a quantitative change in speed of operation, detail of procedure and so on, but the total effect is to bring about a marked qualitative change in the end result.

Any discussion of computers tends to become speculative so let us conclude on a realistic note. Education has rarely had the feedback it requires and progress has consequently been needlessly slow. Computer systems give real hopes of providing the necessary information. They will certainly teach the individual student sensitively and respond to his difficulties, but they are ideal for providing a human teacher with the detailed specifications for rewriting material. In the everyday course of their operations they will record, say, relative speeds of teaching in the initial and later stages of a subject, how frequently material needed rehearsal, how often the same error persisted, whether a shortened version did in fact save time and whether subsequent understanding of material was sufficient. Alternative methods may be objectively assessed and this may apply equally to the work of a human teacher. Teaching may remain an art but there is no reason why it should not have a lot more information on which to base its efforts.

Above all let us be clear on one issue. The fundamental query is not so much what computers can do but what we want them to do. And today in education we must face whether we know enough to answer that question.

CHAPTER 10

SOCIAL IMPLICATIONS OF AN EFFECTIVE TECHNOLOGY

IN this final chapter we wish to consider some of the implications of introducing teaching machines procedures. We expect them to have wide repercussions upon teaching practice, and in their turn we expect improved teaching methods to have wide repercussions upon society. Some of these effects do not appear to have been foreseen. We will begin with some immediate reactions and then turn to wider considerations.

WHAT STUDENTS SAY

In education we are used to the idea that everyone is entitled to his opinion and will undoubtedly give it. We have already argued that students' responses are an integral part of programmed instruction so let us begin with them.

We regard the student as the essential link in the communication chain; others may come and go, testers, examiners, even teachers, but the whole educational exercise is aimed at the benefit of a student. How then does he react to teaching machine methods?

Of course they are something new and a change is generally welcome. Students do record their appreciation of novelty, and whilst too much weight should never be placed on an effect that will wear off, the methods will always contribute some variety to a teaching course. Other things being equal, the greater variation that can be introduced into our teaching the more likely we can hold the attention of students. Certainly when we asked a group of industrial trainees for their comments they were very much in favour of a programming method that had broken down the subject into small units and was trying to make the material as easy as possible. The method of 'somebody talking from a blackboard and boring you' came in for much heartfelt criticism.

If we may consider a very different group, some university students in a Faculty of Arts tried a programme in the revision of logarithms (this work is reported by J. Hartley in his doctorate thesis, 1964). Here was a heterogeneous group and it was not short of criticism when the programme took longer than was considered necessary – 'Do you have to sound like "Listen with Mother"?' Yet some of the comments were most illuminating. 'None of the material was new to me but I have never really understood it before, and I have now been able to assimilate it at my own speed.' 'I have never understood before the processes behind logs., and what in fact logs. really were.' To counterbalance these favourable observations some commented adversely against taking 'far too long for the amount gained' and three students objected to the format because 'turning the book over (to start at the opposite end) shattered the illusion of rapid progress'.

But programmers are cautious about the favourable comments of students. They know only too well that any method will work for a time, provided it is put over with enthusiasm and belief. The query is how much will it contribute once the honeymoon period is over. The reactions to date suggest that a system, which had much to recommend it in theory, has passed its first trials. Students can use it without difficulty and they can learn from it. The real test now comes when it passes to the second stage of being part of the recognized educational system. Will it then continue to have the same success?

It is here that the student's comments and responses are important. The research worker does not believe that programmes are in any final form and continues both to try out different formats and methods, and to examine whether they might not be used in quite different situations from those originally intended. To this end he experiments with group instruction, mechanized classrooms, attempts to stimulate creative thinking, problem solving, generalizations, transfer of training, and so on. One of the key issues is the actual lay out of a programme and its method of presentation. Early work was almost entirely devoted to frame-writing and the splitting up of material into small units. This was the method by which a student's behaviour might be controlled and reinforcement given. As we have seen, the emphasis has now shifted to the much broader analysis of task material. Programme writing is beginning to be seen as one part of educational technology in which the main purpose is to devise a total system. Within such a system many methods may contribute to the desired goal, but it is the nature of such an empirical approach that the methods can be evaluated. The more generally students use programmed instructions and become familiar with them, the more reliable will be their observations.

WHAT TEACHERS SAY

The other partners in the joint enterprise of teaching, the teachers themselves, are likely to be even more vocal than their students, and they have been so about programmed instruction. We should add, often with good cause; for in the early days of these developments the position was often confused and flamboyant claims were put forward, as if an overnight panacea to the world's teaching problems had suddenly popped up. When the truer picture emerged that here was a method demanding its fair share of toil and search, but one that could be assessed and improved, teachers were prepared to listen and to give it a fair trial. Speaking personally we have been in this field of research from its beginning in Britain and in general we have been impressed by the willingness of the teaching profession to consider it. Many a teacher to our knowledge has slaved away on his own at night writing and making up his own programme material, often with no backing at all from any educational authority.

Of course there are objections. This is to be expected of anything new, and there did seem to be something sinister in the early claims for teaching machines. The Press soon stated that robots would replace teachers and conjured up pictures of classrooms of students with little iron men in front of them. On the one hand, it seemed as if the teaching profession might be degraded by machines taking over human duties, on the other, that something essential to teaching in the relationship between student and teacher might be arrogantly swept aside. We have listened to many eloquent denunciations of such heresies and would have every sympathy with the viewpoint, if this were in fact likely to happen, which it is not.

It speaks well for the teaching profession that so many are so ready to consider new methods. Often when opposition is expressed it is fervent and eloquent, often there is conviction backed by a life's work that is worthy of every respect. Only occasionally is there the hint that the speaker is protesting too much and revealing his own insecurity about his methods. In the main, opposition is based on a genuine conviction that the personal relationship between teacher and pupil is the permanent influence in teaching and by its means something far more subtle and important can be imparted. Attitudes and values may be communicated and a whole way of life presented. Of course in an ideal situation this is true and no one is trying to minimize its significance. What programmed instruction is trying to do is to provide a means whereby efficient teaching may take place with clearly defined objectives. This must be invaluable for it is axiomatic that with our present educational system any good teacher is overburdened. His class is too big; he has to teach too often and his responsibilities are too wide. Anything that gives him the opportunity to make more contact with his pupils, that relieves him of the responsibility of teaching some topics or some students at certain points so that he may devote himself to others is desirable. It allows him the flexibility that too often an over-crammed timetable with over-sized classes does not.

Again we have spoken as if all personal influences of staff upon students were beneficial, but this is far from the case. It is a well-nigh universal experience that everyone had some teacher whom they revered and who taught them well and was respected; but alas, it is also common enough to find that there was some representative whom they heartily disliked if not hated, and from whom they learned little. It has to be accepted that often personal relations do sour a pupil's judgement of a subject; the teacher symbolizes his subject and too often it is liked or disliked accordingly. In the negative instances it would be only too beneficial for some objective method to take over and restore the balance. A common example that we have in the university is a girl's dislike of statistics because she disliked mathematics at school. Programmes are invaluable here for often it seems there is no basic inability to understand mathematics but an unfortunate heritage from a subject that has been notoriously inadequately staffed in girls' High Schools in this country.

One objection that teachers make is that the programme attempts to make learning too easy. It goes to great lengths to try to surmount all possible hurdles and explain every anticipated problem of a student. But, it is objected, this is no preparation for life. A student must be trained to think for himself, to meet difficulties on his own and overcome them. There is a great deal in this spirited point but where does it get us? – life is a battle and we need as many practice fights as possible to prepare for it. But training today is not quite so rugged. In the field of athletics we believe in carefully building up a man's strength to face his day of competition. It is surely obvious that when we look around at our educational athletes many students hardly got started in the race. We find our engineering apprentices cannot use fractions, whilst spelling is an unknown skill at any level. Experience would lead us to guess that eighty to ninety per cent of the population cannot spell psychology and that nearly half the population of university students write proffessor for professor. Whatever our feelings about the art of spelling, this is surely no way to teach a major subject such as arithmetic. We do not want casualties, we want successes in terms of students who *understand* what is happening in simple additive and multiplicative adventures.

Let us get our aims clear on this point. No teacher is complimented because he makes his subject more difficult than another. 'Let me introduce Mr X. He can make algebra as unintelligible as any man I know.' We do not make friends by greetings of this kind, and yet to hear some teachers talk it might be thought we do. The fact is that the simpler and more penetrating the teacher can make his explanation, the more his students will understand and – this is the nub of the matter – the farther they will advance in the subject. There are frontiers looming up for all of us in all subjects, but one aim of education is to take each one of us as close as possible to them, whether that frontier be the simple addition of two fractions or a translation of the Dead Sea Scrolls.

We are saying, then, that programming is not attempting to make learning easy for its own sake but because it will enable a student to make progress where otherwise he would not. As we argued in Chapter 5, programmes do not aim to teach students so that they complete the course with the same rank order as their own I.Q.'s. Provided the subject matter is within the student's mental competence the aim is for all to understand at the highest possible level. This may seem too ambitious, but consider the following extract from a government report. 'A good teacher will break down material into digestible units of information, ensure participation of students through questioning, reward correct responses by approval and concentrate on the slower learners.' No doubt a good teacher will do so, with his overcrowded class of forty plus, and no doubt the good teacher will achieve the high level of comprehension that we have mentioned. But any average programme will do this as a matter of course, and also ensure that the slower learners have their opportunity to respond. It is because of this all-round attention to all students that it achieves such a high level of success.

But the outstanding point here seems to be the success that has been achieved where programmed instruction has been integrated into normal teaching courses. Here it has been able to provide some variety of instruction, it has relieved the teacher of part of his routine classwork so that he has more time to devote to personal supervision and it has ensured that every student can take advantage of detailed and evaluated preparation of the subject matter. Where the programme is included as part of the course and is being used by the teacher as an adjunct to his teaching there is no doubt that this powerful technique creates an atmosphere of purpose and progress. In our discussions with teachers who have used the method it is clear that this is more than beginners' enthusiasm: this is confidence both of success and the satisfaction of being able to do a difficult job well.

REACTIONS TO AN EFFICIENT EDUCATIONAL TECHNOLOGY

In the sense that we are, or should be, concerned about the fate of future generations we all have the responsibility of parents. We all profess to be eager to do what is right by our children. Yet the appalling fact is that the man in the street is not interested in education. Education is not even paid the compliment of being taken seriously. If ever a system were condemned it is our present educational method by the complete apathy it has engendered in such large sections of the population. Educators talk endlessly about education but it is a dead subject to past consumers, and only flickers into a brief life when, as parents, they face its failures again with their own children. How well the politicians know this. Cynically they point to the amount being spent on education and how rare it is to get a first-class man appointed to and *staying* at the Ministry of Education. It is the temporary job on the political ladder, in spite of the enormous budget of the Ministry.

The point is that we have come to accept from our educational and training efforts an astonishingly low return, and even an unknown return. We have examinations and it is taken for granted that if the student passes them it is sufficient. Rarely does the general public ask anything about why is this curriculum being taught, what is its aim, what is being missed?

But this could change if we once had a system where results were more evident. Suppose we accept that the new technology of education will one day devise teaching systems which are really efficient at their job. The implications are quite startling. Would we welcome them, or would they in fact create a whole set of new problems. Would they be just a further example of science never solving problems but creating better ones. At the moment we have the uneasy feeling that education is being saved from criticism mainly because of its own inefficiency. We do not need to be afraid of it because, with a few notable exceptions, our schools seem incapable of influencing many of their students. Our public school system in Britain probably turns out more than a random sample of conservatively minded young men, who are rather class conscious. But does it aim to do this? or does it aim to turn out critically minded youngsters who can think for themselves? Our state education in its results is indubitably much more impartial – it continues to produce generations of students who could hardly care less about political thought. But supposing this *status quo* were rudely shattered by an educational technology that was efficient and directed. Any reader who feels doubtful has only to reflect on some of the examples of what happens when methods are applied ruthlessly. It is not chance that there are more young Communists in Russia than the United States.

What happens when a real effort is made to influence the thinking of people? Let us take what will be a shocking example in a discussion on educational methods and consider that most dedicated of professions, advertising. Dare any one of us say that the last purchases we made were in no way influenced by its efforts? Is there not a very real possibility that we have just bought something because its brand image has been conditioned to become part of our thinking? We realize that advertising is subtly influencing our lives with its infiltration into our private thoughts, its suggestions to our ego and its eye-demanding symbols. And of course this may not be happening to us personally, but it certainly happens to our neighbours!

All this is most deplorable, regrettable. And this is not education – this is propaganda, indoctrination, persuasion. But why does it achieve so much success and why are we so opposed to it? Are we just using emotive words about an opposition's educational methods? These harsh suggestions are worth formulating because we have so rarely asked them of our own educational methods. We have had no need. Success has been so infrequent. But once we have an efficient educational system it would raise ethical questions of this kind. We fear a system that is powerful in pursuing objectives which do not always coincide with our own. We would not be afraid of a health service that kept us all perfectly healthy; but we might not accept a strong police service that never allowed us to break the law. Similarly we might welcome a machine that could teach us all to be accident-free drivers by speaking to us while we were asleep. But what if someone changed the record so as to make us all accept a particular political system? We hardly worry about these methods because we are not accustomed to their success, but we may well change our attitude when we appreciate their possibilities.

But irrespective of their success or failure, the ethical problems behind them are the same. The argument is that our educational system saves us from the anxiety of worrying about such issues because of its general inefficiency. It is not going to influence anyone very much so it need not be paid the compliment of being taken seriously. We may well find that this is not so in the future. And we may well find that a number of questions that should have been raised long ago, will suddenly be in the forefront of our discussion. For example, why are we teaching certain subjects? Why are we not teaching others? Why does present-day education give such a hopeless training for the present-day environment? Is there any reason at all behind the present curriculum? When so little is being achieved we can afford to have a '1066 and All That' attitude to history and to any other subject, but does any one seriously believe now that the choice of everyday school subjects is satisfactory? How does it equip a young student to understand his world? What does it teach him about society, its structure, its organization as a community? What does it tell him about himself as an individual, as an organism with all the fascinating complexities of an inherited nervous system that has developed over the millennia?

This attitude of apathy may change once it is realized that more can be achieved. Parents are apt to pay attention only to examination results. If little Willy gets through his examinations then 'God's in His heaven, and all's right with Education.' Maybe! But a generation that was once educated to come to grips with the arts and problems of living in its present world might come to expect different standards from education, as it is now demanding higher standards in its home surroundings, its communication systems and the like. Educational standards would only be following in the wake of many others.

NOT ENOUGH INTELLIGENCE TO GO ROUND

One last point. It is a sad statistical fact, periodically discovered by some letter writer to *The Times*, that half the population of any normally distributed variable will be below average. The implications of this fact apparently fluctuate. It is not startling, for example, that half the human population will be below average height. But when applied to intelligence the implications have a more sinister ring – half the population are below average intelligence. To what are we condemning them? The answer is definite – to education! to training!

We are living in a community where the number of jobs that do not demand education and training is steadily diminishing. Lift attendants disappear as automatic lifts replace them but for every twenty lifts we want another technician, and so on. We cannot manufacture brains – yet – for such jobs. We can train for them and we can systematize that training so that personnel who would never have been thought capable of taking on such work will do so. We have no alternative. There is not enough intelligence to go round. This is the rarely admitted fact of present civilization. And we are bumping against this datum point at every turn. It is not true that it has always been a limitation. For centuries communities existed on an army of under-privileged servants and lackeys whose lives were intolerable and would have been worse had they been more intelligent. Slave labour built the pyramids and the early civilizations. To some degree efficiency depended upon a lack of intelligence. Now many western states have reversed this position with responsible jobs for the majority and we are desperately looking around for the brains we have not got. Every step towards automation takes the community nearer to the point where each individual will have to do some thinking for himself, either at his work or in his increasing leisure time. It would seem to be another clear indication where we shall be calling upon machines to redress the balance – this time to teach men in new subjects and new techniques, and indeed in the older art of thinking for himself.

THE REDISTRIBUTION OF MANPOWER

The shortage of intelligence is nowhere more acute than in teaching. We are always slow to face up to long-term problems, but this one has caught up with us now as never before. There are only a few, proportionately a very limited few, who can teach the more advanced subjects that it is necessary to teach in a highly developed technological community. The teaching profession has argued, and it is very understandable, for equality among its staff members. To teach a five-year-old is as important as a fifteen-year-old. Of course it is. But, and this is the rub, it is not so demanding on brain-power. To understand the five-year-old may be exceptionally difficult, but to control and teach him may be more a demand on patience than intellect. Hitler may have run short of patience but fortunately it is a quality than many ordinary mortals do possess. We are arguing that we are desperately short of brains, and we must be prepared to pay for them. We need to back them up by every *support service* that is possible. In Britain we do just the reverse – we appoint university professors and then expect them to carry out the duties of secretaries and animal attendants.

But even when we get the support services in perspective we shall still be short of top-level teachers. And to this end we must now begin reorganizing. There is little enthusiasm in Britain at any governmental level for promoting research into developing these methods. At this moment there is no sustained research scheme into computer teaching techniques. Yet the argument that computer teaching will come in the next decade seems irrefutable to us on the data we now have. On the one hand we have the ever-increasing sum total of knowledge; it is growing at a rate that has never been so rapid. On the other there is the increasing size of world populations that have to know such information. We not only need to make every effort to spread our advanced knowledge to more individuals, but equally we have to raise the educational level of large masses of our population if they are to carry out their industrial role in the future, and we are deluding ourselves if we think we have any choice in the matter. All this adds up to a huge increase in the demand for teaching. We need to teach to survive. It is our only way of providing the means to the end, that is, a population that is more highly educated and with the technical knowledge to enjoy the potential advantages of a modern community. The means – education – does not guarantee the end – the full and satisfying life – but we do know that without it the end is impossible. The challenge, then, is to design educational systems whereby we can teach our communities to live, to think, and to learn at a higher level than they have done at any time in recorded history. This is the quiet revolution; a non-sensational affair yet offering a fundamental challenge to us – how the major part of a community may come to live as human beings. We have now within our grasp the tools to help us as never before, yet we are showing neither insight nor enthusiasm for this work. The quiet revolution may well come in spite of our lack of foresight. Certainly its success is our biggest hope for the future.

INDEX

PSYCHOLOGY OF CHILDHOOD AND ADOLESCENCE

C. I. Sandström

In this concise study of the processes of growing up Professor Sandström has produced a book which, although it is perfectly suited to the initial needs of university students and teachers in training, will appeal almost as much to parents and ordinary readers. His text covers the whole story of human physical and mental growth from conception to puberty.

Outlining the scope and history of developmental psychology, Professor Sandström goes on to detail the stages of growth in the womb, during the months after birth, and (year by year) up to the age of ten. There follow chapters on physical development, learning and perception, motivation, language and thought, intelligence, the emotions, social adjustment, and personality. The special conditions of puberty and of schooling are handled in the final chapters.

Throughout this masterly study the author necessarily refers to 'norms of development': these neatly represent the average stages of growing up, but (as Professor Mace comments in his introduction) they must only be applied to individual children with caution.

CONTRARY IMAGINATIONS

A Psychological Study of the English Schoolboy

Liam Hudson

Why does one boy become an arts specialist and his neighbour a scientist? Why do some pupils use their brains effectively and others not? Do we pay enough attention to personality in assessing ability?

In this controversial study Dr Liam Hudson, Director of the Research Unit on Intellectual Development at King's College, Cambridge, argues that personality counts for as much as ability in the student's choice of subject. He distinguishes between two types of personality, the scientific 'converger' and the artistic, imaginative 'diverger', and examines examples of each in depth. He then speculates on the nature of original thought, and the ways in which intellectual and personal qualities interact. His argument combines the disciplines of intelligence testing and psycho-analysis in a highly original way, and his clear and jargon-free presentation will appeal to all those interested in intelligent children, in psychology, or in both.